Our Own Path t

Our Own Path to Socialism

Selected Speeches of Hugo Chávez

Edited by
Carlos Ron
Manolo De Los Santos
Vijay Prashad

First published in January 2023 by
1804 Books at The People's Forum, New York, NY
in association with
LeftWord Books, New Delhi, India

1804books.com

This selection and English translation © 1804 Books at
The People's Forum, New York, NY

ISBN: 978-1-7368500-6-0

Contents

Foreword   7
   by Jorge Arreaza
The Luminous Theories of Hugo Chávez   11
   by Carlos Ron, Manolo De Los Santos, and Vijay Prashad
We are on that path!   23
   Speech in the Aula Magna of the University of Havana on December 14, 1994 – Havana, Cuba
Transcending capitalism   34
   Speech at the closing of the World Social Forum on January 30, 2005 – Porto Alegre, Brazil
This is called socialism   54
   Speech at the Inauguration on January 10, 2007 – Caracas, Venezuela
The communes and the construction of socialism   74
   Speech during Aló Presidente *at the Teresa Carreño Theater on June 11, 2009 – Caracas, Venezuela*
Join the side of socialism   88
   Speech at the UN General Assembly on September 24, 2009 – New York, United States
Only through the path of socialism   104
   Speech at the XV UN Climate Change Conference on December 16, 2009 – Copenhagen, Denmark
Strike at the helm   113
   Speech at the Council of Ministers at the Miraflores Palace on October 20, 2012 – Caracas, Venezuela
Glossary   128
Contributors   136

Foreword

Jorge Arreaza

"We remember Comandante Chávez's speech in Porto Alegre, Brazil, where he pronounced the words that are the compass of the Revolution: Socialism is the only path to social equality. That is the Path! Always with the people, guaranteeing the Supreme Social Happiness." – Nicolás Maduro

A HURRICANE HAS SWEPT through Latin America since 1999. Just when there were multiple attempts to impose the Washington Consensus on the peoples of the world, the Venezuelan people elected Hugo Chávez to lead the destiny of a process that wasn't only a protest against neoliberalism. Chávez would lead a Latin Americanist national project rooted in the Global South and filled with the glorious history of the struggles for independence, a deeply rooted Venezuelan identity, and an unwavering commitment to social justice that demonstrated that another horizon and another reality was possible in the face of capitalism.

Comandante Hugo Chávez's deep connection with his people allowed him to interpret both the needs and the desires of the Venezuelan working class. He broke with the *caudillo* type of leadership, which traditionally only defended its own particular or partisan interests without truly raising the banners of anti-imperialism, anti-colonialism, or the possibility of making structural changes in society. Chávez, rather, trusted the Venezuelan people's capacity to take power and become agents of their own transformation. All his efforts, from the summoning of a plenipotentiary National Constituent Assembly to draft a new Constitution to the promotion and creation of communes, were strategic wagers to generate the birth and the strengthening of People's Power.

Chávez's legacy today rests on a series of pillars that constitute the Bolivarian Revolution – the construction of a participatory and protagonist democracy; the wager on a multipolar and multicentric world; the defense of the State and the sovereignty of the Nation and of its natural resources; the democratization of access to information; and the civilian-military unity, all essential elements in the formulation of the Bolivarian Socialism of the 21st Century – a rescue, without dogmatism or finished formulas, of the historical struggles of the peoples, adapted to the realities of Venezuela, of Latin America and the conjuncture of the 21st century.

Some of us who were swept away by the hurricane that is the Bolivarian Revolution were fortunate to directly receive from the Comandante his guidance, his advice, his reflections, and even his scoldings. Still, a whole generation of youth is educating itself in the heat of the greatest aggression that Venezuela has suffered from imperialism in 200 years, who were unable to have that closeness with our giant. These young people must read him, study him, debate him, and above all, ask themselves daily how to follow his example to guarantee the irreversibility of the Revolution.

This compilation is one of many tools we must put in the hands of the Venezuelan youth and young people worldwide with an internationalist calling. It's important that they may know, from his voice, the Chávez who opened the doors of a South American revolution, who wasn't afraid to say that the only way to overcome capitalism is socialism, and that "it is possible to transcend capitalism through the way of socialism in democracy." Chávez motivated us to be anti-imperialist from our Bolivarian, anti-colonialist, and Indo-African American roots. He taught us to think, see ourselves, and act as a People, to fight until our last breath for the People's Power, for the commune, and for a Bolivarian socialism, of concrete utopias, deeply humanist, egalitarian, and ethical, Latin Americanist and multipolar, whose goal is shared social happiness.

Returning to Comandante Chávez's ideas is necessary for a Venezuela that is going through a new era of transition to socialism. It is also necessary for a world in which Covid-19 demonstrated that the capitalist system is involved in a crisis to which it will not be able to adapt and for which it no longer has solutions for the majority of humanity. While we face the resurgence of hatred, our world needs other moral, social, economic, and ideological referents to save the planet. In Chávez and his word, we have our most crucial referent.

May this compendium of speeches be, therefore, an instrument of resistance and a constant rebirth of our practices, of our actions, and of the battle of ideas; but, above all, may it inspire us to continue revolutionizing what exists to definitively disarm neoliberal capitalism, to put an end to exploitation and all the expressions of imperialism, to consolidate a path in democracy, to live with dignity and better every day. In today's Venezuela, under the leadership of President Nicolás Maduro and the United Socialist Party of Venezuela, after six years of brutal imperialist aggression, the theory and praxis of Hugo Chávez is an essential guide, reference, and the main path of the Consolidation of the Bolivarian Revolution. Reading, studying, analyzing, criticizing, and feeling the ideas and emotions of Comandante Chávez must become a necessity for the new generations in their unstoppable impulse to build an alternative, humane and egalitarian future.

Chávez Vive!

The Luminous Theories of Hugo Chávez

Carlos Ron, Manolo De Los Santos, and Vijay Prashad

HUGO RAFAEL CHÁVEZ FRIAS (1954-2013) lit up a stage like few people. He would stride onto the stage, his eyes darting from one end of the room or the avenue, making contact with this person and then that person, making every person in the room feel as if they were intimately connected to him. Chávez was not a tall man – five feet six inches – but his personality did not require height. The people cheered with abandon, feeling his presence there not as someone separate from them but as their representative, as the person who represented their lives and their feelings, their aspirations for the future of their country and the world. Chávez. That was their cry. Chávez. It was enough.

On 27 February 1989, the people who lived in the slums around Caracas, Venezuela took to the streets against an arbitrary rise in petrol prices. The city was lost to the government, as ordinary people inflicted their anger on a government that seemed to have its finance minister on a permanent hotline to the International Monetary Fund headquarters. The elimination of petrol subsidies for a country that has one of the largest deposits of petroleum seemed beyond reason to people whose budgets had been corralled to the task of national debt-servicing rather than their own humanity. The government of Carlos Andrés Pérez responded with characteristic brutality: over three thousand people are estimated to have been killed in the melee that followed his suspension of crucial constitutional protections to the people and the military response. Soldiers from the same rural and slum backgrounds as the protestors were forced to fire to kill.

An officer at the National Security and Defense Council at the presidential Miraflores Palace, Hugo Chávez, was on sick leave during what came to be called *El Caracazo* (also *Sacudón*, the day that shook the country). He returned after the cordite had cleared. His troops told him that they were sickened by the orders to shoot at their own people. Never again, they said to Chávez.

Like most of his troops, Chávez came from the impoverished countryside, from Venezuela's *llanos*, flatlands. His parents were schoolteachers who sent two of their seven children to live with a grandmother, Rosa. Rosa's Catholicism and the poverty of their lives marked the two boys, Adán and Hugo – the elder would become a physicist and a clandestine member of the Partido Revolucionario Venezolano (PRV), whose leader Douglas Bravo took Che Guevara's *foco* strategy to Venezuela; the latter, Hugo, would join the military, as did so many of his childhood friends. There were few avenues for mobility from the flatlands, with the military being the main path for young men. Chávez benefitted from the entry of a nationalistic curriculum into the military and from his encounters with the Peruvian leftist General Juan Velasco Alvarado and with leftist Panamanian General Omar Torrijos. Experiences with the harsh counter-insurgency operations of the military against the guerrillas led Chávez in search of an alternative. He set up the Bolivarian Revolutionary Movement as a clandestine unit inside the armed forces. In the early 1980s, Chávez met with Bravo who later recalled, "We did not envisage an immediate uprising, we were clear about that. [We] agreed that unless there was a significant political development in the country – a 'sense of expectation in the mass of the people' – nothing much would happen until the military conspirators were senior enough to have command of troops."

After the *Caracazo*, Lieutenant Colonel Chávez put into motion the plots sketched out by his left-wing conspiracy within the military. Operation Zamora, the military rebellion of 1992 failed, and Chávez was arrested. Chávez asked to address the people on television to call off the rebellion. It was a mistake to let him go near a television set. Chávez made two points. First, he took personal responsibility for the event – something unheard of in Venezuelan politics ("I alone shoulder the responsibility for this Bolivarian military uprising"). Second, he pointed out that for now, *por ahora*, the uprising had been suspended. The nature of the military rebellion's failure raised the stature of Chávez and his co-conspirators. During his two years in Yare prison, with his legal team (led by Cilia Flores, the wife of Chávez's successor Nicolas Maduro), Chávez worked to build a civilian movement.

Chávez turned to the older currents of the organized Left, including the Communists, the social democrats, and the guerrillas, and to the working-class leaders, such as the bus driver union head Luís Miquilena (who would establish the Patriotic Front based on the energy of the *Caracazo*). He absorbed the revolutionary heritage of his country, with the three 19th-century rebels anchoring his imagination – Simón Bolívar, Simón Rodríguez, and Ezequiel Zamora. It was from Zamora that Chávez drew the three aspects of his ideology: (1) *Horror a la oligarquía* (Hatred toward the oligarchy); (2) *Elección popular* (General elections); (3) *Tierra y hombres libres* (Land and free people). These principles anchored the Bolivarian Revolutionary Movement (MBR-200), the political platform for Chávez and his allies.

Released from prison in 1994, Chávez and the MBR-200 earned the support of the Movement for Socialism (MAS) and *La Causa*

R, two of the main left political formations in Venezuela. The 1998 presidential elections beckoned, and Chávez expressed interest in it. His supporters created a new organization, *Movimiento Quinta República* (MVR), the movement of the Fifth Republic, and as the election neared all manner of progressive groups and parties came to Chávez's side, to his *Polo Patriótico*, the Patriotic Pole. Chávez's bloc won 56.2 percent of the vote, sending him to Miraflores Palace for the first of three terms (he won a fourth term in October 2012, but died before he could take the helm once more). A desiccated political landscape in the 1990s thrust Chávez forward as the leader of the new dynamic. His immense charisma, earthy charm, and frank disdain for the old ruling classes endeared him to the ordinary people – whose adoration of him was seen often on the streets of Venezuela.

Chávez's victory was a blow to the ruling class, which had not only monopolized political power, but it has absorbed the fruits of Venezuela's oil economy. Subservience to the United States had become habit, which is why the class now turned toward Washington as Chávez began to build on the momentum of his elections. They would fight Chávez and the Bolivarian movement at every turn, including through a failed *coup d'etat* attempt in 2002. Washington saw Chávez as the main enemy, and when George W. Bush came to office, he turned his gun on the Bolivarian revolution. It was Chávez's victory that opened the Pink Tide, reconciling revolutionary and electoral politics, bringing forth a transformation in Latin America – from military dictatorships and neo-liberal autocracies, the continent now elected one left-wing leader after another. They looked to Chávez for inspiration, as he would in turn look to the resilient example of Cuba's Fidel Castro for encouragement (the first speech in this collection is from the visit of Chávez to Havana in 1994, when he first met Fidel). It is no wonder that the US government saw

Chávez as the principal enemy. In June 2007, US deputy assistant Secretary of State for Western Hemispheric Affairs, Craig Kelly, wrote a confidential memorandum to the CIA, the Pentagon, and the State Department. Kelly outlined the means to limit Chávez's "influence" and "reassert US leadership in the region." Chávez, he wrote, is a "formidable foe", but "he certainly can be taken." These were ominous words, which showed both how dangerous Chávez was to US hegemony in the region and to what lengths the US and its Venezuelan allies proposed to go against him.

The counter-revolutionary tendencies led by the Venezuelan oligarchy and directed by Washington did not weaken the resolve of Chávez and the Bolivarian revolution; in fact, the pressure campaign only radicalized the revolution. Chávez had moved slowly after the 1998 election, but as he began to be attacked more and more, he used that energy to deepen the revolutionary processes.

Throughout the 1990s, different progressive political processes emerged in Latin America that questioned and challenged neoliberal hegemony. Yet the Venezuelan process with Hugo Chávez and the Bolivarian Revolution dramatically altered the region's geopolitical situation in favor of the working class by taking the dust off and bringing back the specter of socialism in public discourse. It was often in the heat of Hugo Chávez's speeches to workers, communal leaders, or the UN General Assembly that he would often seek to define the meaning of "Socialism in the 21st Century."

Chávez spoke about "Socialism in the 21st Century" as a model that was not simply in contrast to the socialisms of the 20th century but, in the current context of neoliberal domination, would need to address economic transformation, democratic participation, and regional integration with a socialism that could not copy past models but instead had to make a "heroic creation" of its own (quoting the Peruvian Marxist José Carlos Mariátegui). This heroic creation of socialism needed to incorporate the traditions of the historical Latin American movements for independence and national liberation that have their origin in what Chavez called the "tree of the three roots" what he considered to be the greatest thinkers and revolutionaries of Latin America and Venezuela: Simón Rodríguez, Simón Bolívar, and Ezequiel Zamora, from whom he recovers the ideas of regionalism, Latin American unity, dignity, and sovereignty for the people. Chávez recognized the legacy of the Venezuelans' past struggles for their liberation and the need to recover this historical memory. The road to socialism in Venezuela has its roots in the legacy of the men and women who joined the armies of liberation and freed the continent.

In the same way, Hugo Chávez did not only recover these heroes of independence for socialism but also incorporated among its sources, essential elements from the traditions of Left and Marxist thought of the 19th and 20th centuries in Latin America, such as the thought of José Martí and Mariátegui, along with the legacy of the triumphant socialist revolutions in the Soviet Union, China, Korea, and Cuba.

> We cannot ignore that contribution and the experience of the Soviet Revolution, the Chinese Revolution, the Cuban Revolution, much closer to us in space and time, in character and roots. That's why you must study a lot. You must read a lot, discuss, and read the socialist theses, and from that accumulation of knowledge, invent Socialism with Venezuelan characteristics in this time and this place.

Chávez also introduced in his conception of socialism a heavy emphasis on recognizing the limits of bourgeois democracy to build a new participatory democracy with the working class as the main protagonist. The creation of new political and institutional bodies of popular participation and new channels of closeness and collaboration with the state allowed for a radically new interaction in the process and decision-making of political affairs.

A constant reference for Chávez is also of the Patria Grande as the basis for a socialist future and democratic international order, often appealing to the need for peace, justice, and equality among the peoples of the Americas. Only under new relations of solidarity could Latin America form a bloc that, while respecting the sovereignty of each nation, could also build a common strength to be on an equal footing with other regions and denounce or resist neocolonialist and imperialist domination. Chávez called on the peoples of the world to look at the future of a democratic international order in strengthening regional blocs against US imperialist unipolarity.

Chávez's Bolivarian movement, building from his dynamic understanding of "Socialism in the 21st Century", undertook four kinds of basic reforms in the country:

1. Constitutional

When Chávez was sworn in 1999, he did so on what he called the "moribund constitution", one written by the old oligarchy in their image. He called for a constitutional process, through a referendum, to write a new constitution that better reflected the values of his new constituency, the vast mass of the Venezuelan people, the workers and peasants, the Afro-Venezuelans, and the Amerindians. An astonishing 88 percent of the population voted for a new constitution. Between 1811 and 1961, Venezuela had twenty-six constitutions, with the oil oligarchy's 1961 document lasting for the longest duration, till 1999. Chávez went to the new constituent assembly to remind them of their task:

> Our existing laws are disastrous relics derived from every despotic regime there has ever been, both ancient and modern; let us ensure that this monstrous edifice will collapse and

crumble, so that we may construct a temple of justice away from its ruins, and dictate a new Venezuelan legal code under the influence of its sacred inspiration.

The new constitution enshrined progressive values at its head – women's rights, human rights, health rights, education rights, employment rights ("Every worker has the right to a sufficient salary that allows a life with dignity and covers his own and his family's basic material, social, and intellectual necessities"), indigenous rights, environmental rights, and, finally, the right to civil disobedience ("people of Venezuela ... disavow any regime, legislation, or authority that contradicts the values, principles, and democratic guarantees or impairment of human rights"). This was one of the most radical constitutions in the world.

2. Control over oil wealth

The new social agenda could not be established without government control over the oil wealth. Venezuela's far-sighted oil minister of the 1950s, and architect of OPEC, Perez Alfonzo called oil the "devil's excrement," the thick sludge that created more inequality despite its lucrativeness. Chávez's government nationalized the oil company, renegotiated the rent prices (through the 2001 Hydrocarbons Law), and removed the layer of corrupt officialdom from the spigot. The exchequer was able to earn a greater percentage of the royalties from the multinational oil firms. The oil company set up its own Social Development Fund (Fondespa) to finance schemes for oil workers, their communities, and other projects (including the provision of below-market oil sales to comradely countries, such as Cuba, and to poor communities of the United States and Western Europe). The oil wealth was now to be used to industrialize the country, to prevent Venezuela to remain dependent on its oil sales and on the import of everything. Diversification of the economy was a key part of the Bolivarian agenda, including the revival of the country's agriculture. This was a consistent theme of Chávez' speeches.

3. Social well-being of the population

It was because of that oil money that Chávez's government could increase social spending by 61 percent ($772 billion). But this money was not turned over as individual transfer payments. It was used carefully to harness the social lives of the population. The Chávez government set up various *misiones* (missions) – along the grain of the rights enshrined in the 1999 constitution. For example, in 2003 the government set up three missions (Robinson, Ribas, and Sucre) to send educators into low-income areas to provide free literacy and higher education courses. The Mission Zamora took in hand the process of land reform, and the Mission Vuelta al Campo sought to encourage people to return to the countryside from the slumlands of the cities. Mission Mercal provided low-cost high-quality food to help wean the population off highly processed imported foodstuff, while the Mission Barrio Adentro sought to provide low-cost, high-quality medical care to the working class and poor.

It was through the work of these Missions that Venezuela's people saw a decline in poverty rates by 37.6 percent from 1999 to the present (the decline of extreme poverty is stunning: from 16.6 percent in 1999 to 7 percent in 2011, a 57.8 percent decline; if you begin the measurement from 2004, when the Missions had begun to have an impact, the decline is by 70 percent). Venezuela, one of the harshest unequal social orders prior to 1999, became one of the least unequal societies; the Gini coefficient dropped by 54 percent, indicating the impact that these basic social policies have had on everyday life.

As the revolutionary process radicalized, Chávez turned from the provision of social goods through the *misiones* to the construction of communes as the social basis for production and consumption of goods. In 2005, Chávez told the National Assembly that there was a need to transform "the economic model, increasing cooperativism, collective property, the submission of private property to the social interest and to the general interest." Such a transformation, he argued, must be created "from the popular bases, with the participation of the communities, through community organizations, the cooperatives, self-management, and different ways to create this system." His speech in 2009, collected here, is a key text to understand the role of the communes in revolutionary Venezuela.

4. Regionalism

From early into his political career, Chávez recognized the importance of a regional solution to South America's malaise. This is why the central icon was Bolivar, the leader whose military prowess helped liberate the continent from Spain (he is known as The Liberator). Chávez moved to build alliances with the new left-tide in the region, as well as to put pressure on US clients to accede to what had become clear was a new reality: a regional politics with the US on the side-lines.

Chávez led the move to scuttle the US-pushed neoliberal Free Trade Area of the Americas (2005) and replaced that momentum with the Bolivarian Alliance for the Peoples of Our America (ALBA) – this would build on the petro-diplomacy of Venezuela (through Petrocaribe and Petrosur) and the trade alliance forged between Venezuela and Cuba (2004). It was to lead to modest monetary linkages, through the BancoSur and the virtual currency, the *Sucre*. The Chávez government moved a cultural agenda, through a regional television channel (TeleSUR) and exchanges across the hemisphere, to build close people-to-people ties as the human face of the economic arrangements.

By 2010, the unity of the hemisphere culminated in the creation, at the initiative of Brazil, of the Community of Latin American and Caribbean States (CELAC), which, unlike the Organization of American States (1948), no longer had the United States as a member. ALBA and CELAC underlined the end of US primacy in the region, a consequence of Chávez's Bolivarian agenda. Even the main US client in the region, Colombia, had to join CELAC much to the chagrin of Washington.

These four elements are important parts of the theory of Chávez' Bolivarian revolution and of "Socialism in the 21st Century." He left behind thousands of hours of speeches and thousands of pages of documents and reports. Some of these texts are available in the six-volume selection made by the Venezuelan government in 2005, and others are collected in innumerable selections from his writings and speeches produced by a range of publishers across Latin America. This volume offers a modest selection, only seven speeches from 1994 to 2012, and only those that we consider to be emblematic of the theory of Chávez' Bolivarianism. It does not attempt to be a comprehensive selection or even a definitive one. It is designed to be studied by those who are interested in the way Chávez thought about the Bolivarian revolutionary project, to learn – in other words – how to think like Chávez.

It is impossible to capture the words of Chávez on the page. When he spoke, he would often break into song, a line from Alí Primera here or from a *ranchera* (as he did when he sang along with Vicente Fernández. When he left prison in 1994, he was asked by a journalist if he had a message for the Venezuelan people. "Yes, let them listen to Alí Primera's songs," he said. Primera's 1975 *Casas de Carton* (Cardboard Houses) asked the key questions for Venezuelan socialism: When does the suffering pass? When does hope come? (*¿Cuando pasa el sufrimiento? ¿Cuando viene la esperanza?*). That sensibility of song in the midst of the speech combined with Chávez' reach into the depths of plebian, rustic phrases and stories cannot be easily conveyed in a text such as we have produced. We recommend that you watch his speeches on-line to get the flavor of his cadence and his argument, the resonance of the tremendous poetry of the Venezuelan *llanos*.

Our work here is part of a project to resurrect a tradition of National Liberation Marxism, one that develops as part of the anti-colonial struggle and expands toward the possibility of building socialism in the poorer nations. Chávez is rooted squarely in this tradition, eager as he was to develop a praxis that was rooted in Venezuela but also in the revolutionary possibilities for the world (as he sketched out in his speech at the World Social Forum in 2005). This book, these speeches, are a starting point to develop a more focused understanding of the ideas of *Chavismo*.

Many thanks to all who had a hand in making this book possible. To the publishers and editors at 1804 Books (Layan Fuleihan, Kate Gonzales, and Manu Karuka); as well as to Sudhanva Deshpande and all the friends at LeftWord Books who helped format and design the book, getting it over the finish line. To the staff of the Simón Bolívar Institute (ISB), The People's Forum, Tricontinental: Institute for Social Research; and the comrades of the International People's Assembly for their support and solidarity. To Hannah Craig for designing a wonderful cover that will spark in people a desire to read the words of this modern revolutionary.

And finally, unending gratitude and solidarity to those continuing Chávez's legacy in the Venezuelan struggle against US imperialism. Viva Chávez!

We are on that path!

Speech given at the Aula Magna of the University of Havana on December 14, 1994 – Havana, Cuba.

COMMANDER IN CHIEF OF the Cuban Revolution and President of the Republic of Cuba; Rector of this distinguished house of studies; President of the Federation of University Students; President of the "Simón Bolívar" House;

My dear compatriots, university professors, students of Cuba, of this land of Martí and Bolívar;

Comrades in arms:

First of all, please receive a warm and heartfelt Bolivarian embrace from the Venezuelan land, of which we feel so fulfilled and to which we have committed our entire life.

Last night, on this fleeting but nevertheless profound trip to Cuba, a Cuban compatriot on the plane asked me if it was the first time I had come to Cuba. I said to her: yes. But I also told her something that I want to repeat now, in this very moving moment: it is the first time I have come here physically, because we young Latin Americans have come to Cuba many times in our dreams. We Bolivarian soldiers of the Venezuelan army, who have decided to dedicate our lives to a revolutionary project, a transformative project, have come to Cuba countless times in our dreams.

And so, I am truly grateful for this new honor that President Fidel Castro gives me, that you all give me. Last night, when I had the immense and pleasant surprise of being received at the José Martí International Airport by him in person, I told him, "I don't deserve this honor. I aspire to deserve it in the months and years to come." I say the same to all of you, my dear Cuban-Latin American compatriots. We hope to come one day to Cuba in a position to open our arms and mutually nourish each other with a Latin American revolutionary project. Imbued, as we have been for centuries, with the idea of a Hispanic American, Latin American, Caribbean continent. United as the single nation that we are.

We are on that path. As Aquiles Nazoa said of José Martí, we feel we belong to all times and all places. We walk like the wind behind the seed that fell here one day. Here, in fertile soil, it sprouted and grew as we have always said it would. I do not say this now because I am in Cuba and, as they say in my country, in the Venezuelan *llanos*, because I feel handsome and encouraged, but because we would say this in the Venezuelan army before becoming insurrectionist soldiers. We would say this in the halls of the Venezuelan military schools. Cuba is a bastion of dignity in Latin America. It must be seen as such. We must follow and nurture it as such.

At this moment there is a hurricane of emotions, ideas, passions, and feelings going through my mind and nesting in the soul of a soldier, a revolutionary, a Latin American. So many things gather in my mind, so many memories, so many dreams of Cuba, of being in Cuba. And at last, to be here!

I was remembering, among the many things that come to me at this moment in this Great Hall of the University of Havana, of having read in Yare prison, Comandante Castro, president of Cuba that fiery defense, those blazing words of yours in "History Will Absolve Me." And of also having read in prison "A Grain of Corn," the interview made at that time by the commander Tomás Borges. And of having so many comparisons of so many ideas, with almost 40 years of difference between the two. And to have drawn several conclusions as an imprisoned soldier. One of them being that it is worthwhile and necessary to keep the flag of dignity and principle raised high, even at the risk of being left to stand alone at any moment. To keep the sails high against unfavorable winds. To maintain positions of dignity. We would read and re-read this in prison. For us it was, and still is, food for rebels.

Speaking of rebels, I emphasize what was said by the Commander in Chief Fidel Castro about the Miami summit: that summit was not held for rebels, therefore, Cubans were not there.

We cannot enter North American territory either. They have forbidden us to enter. I said it once in Colombia and I will say it again now, in Cuba, with more force and more vigor: they honor us as rebel soldiers by not allowing us to enter US territory!

There is no doubt that interesting things are happening in Latin America and the Caribbean. There is no doubt that the famous poet and writer of ours, of this America of ours, Pablo Neruda, was absolutely right when he wrote that Bolívar wakes up every 100 years when the people awaken.

There is no doubt that we are in an era of awakenings, of resurrections of peoples, of strength, and of hope. There is no doubt, President, that the wave that you announced and continue announcing in that interview to which I referred, "A Grain of Corn," is sensed and felt throughout all of Latin America.

There is no doubt that we are in the bicentennial era. We had the audacity to establish a movement within the ranks of the Venezuelan National Army. Fed up with so much corruption, we vowed to dedicate our lives to the construction of a revolutionary movement and to the revolutionary struggle in Venezuela and now, in the Latin American context.

We began this in the bicentennial year of Bolívar's birth. This coming year is the centennial of the death of José Martí. This coming year is the bicentennial of the birth of Marshal Antonio José de Sucre. This coming year is the bicentennial of the rebellion and death of José Leonardo Chirinos on the coast of Coro in

Venezuela, the land, by the way, of the ancestors of the hero Antonio Maceo.

As time calls us and impels us, it is undoubtedly time to walk once again along the paths of hope and struggle. That is what we are doing. After 10 years of intense work within the Venezuelan army. After one rebellion and another rebellion, we are now dedicated to revolutionary work in three fundamental directions that I will permit myself to summarize for you in order to invite you to an exchange; to invite you to extend bonds of unity and work, of concrete construction.

In the first place, we are determined to raise an ideological flag that is both pertinent and beneficial to our Venezuelan land and our Latin American land: the Bolivarian flag.

In this ideological work of reviewing the history and ideas that were born in Venezuela and in this continent 200 years ago, when the first project of a nation, not only Venezuelan, but Latin American, was being built – that project that Francisco de Miranda called Colombellay, which Bolívar later called Colombia, and what we know today as the Great Colombia, the Bolivarian dream. In this plunge into history in search of our roots, we have designed and launched for national and international public debate the idea of what we call a "tree of three roots."

The root of Bolivarian thought, of Simon Bolívar, who called for Latin American unity in order to oppose the pretensions of the North, which already clawed at our Latin American land. Bolívar who in Angostura proposed the need to incorporate, in addition to the three classic powers of Montesquieu, a fourth power, a moral power. Bolívar, who proposed a fifth power in the Bolivian Constitution, the electoral power. That Bolívar who, almost in his tomb and already in Santa Marta, said, "The military must take up its sword to defend social guarantees." Bolívar, who said that the best system of government is the one that provides the greatest amount of happiness to its people and the greatest amount of political stability and social security.

We have unified this deep root, this Bolivarian root. It is unified by time and by history itself, to the Robinsonian root, which takes as inspiration the name of Samuel Robinson or Simón Rodríguez, of whom we Latin Americans know very little. He was described as "Bolívar's teacher" to us since we were children, and there he remained as if stigmatized by history, as the bizarre madman who died old, wandering like the wind through the peoples of Latin America.

Simón Rodríguez gave Simón Bolívar much of his revolutionary ideas. Simón Rodríguez, called on the Southern Americans to realize two revolutions: the political and the economic. That Simón Rodríguez called for the construction of a social economy model and a popular economy model. That Simón Rodríguez left, as a challenge for us, the idea that Latin America, at that time termed South America, could not continue to imitate obediently. Rather it must be original and called to invent or to err. That crazy old man, according to the bourgeoisie of the time, went around gathering already older and abandoned children: "Children are the stones of the future edifice of the Republic, come here to polish the stones so that this edifice will be solid and luminous." That old man who, already on the verge of the grave, dedicated himself to making candles, and when someone asked him, "What are you doing making candles, teacher?" he said, "I can't find any other way to give light to America." That is another fundamental, deep and philosophical root of our ideological approach.

And a more recent root is the Zamoran root. Taken from the general of the sovereign people, Ezequiel Zamora. Zamora, leader of the Federal Revolution in Venezuela. Zamora, the general who wore a double head covering, a straw hat and a military kepi over the straw hat, and explained this with a concept that Mao Zedong later reflected in another way, in another time and another place.

Mao pointed out that the people are to the army as water is to the fish. You not only know this; you have applied it. I take this opportunity (excuse the digression) to give a huge embrace, a gigantic embrace to the Revolutionary Armed Forces of Cuba who have identified themselves with their people forever.

In just a few hours we are leaving dear comrades in arms of Cuba, convinced, in spite of the little we were able to see, that you do apply the idea that you are (just like the title of a good work by a Panamanian scholar on the subject) like fish in the water.

We, as military men, follow in this pursuit. Today, we leave more firmly rooted in the conviction and the necessity for the Venezuelan army to be once again what it was. An army of the people, an army to defend what Bolívar called social guarantees.

Ezequiel Zamora, who I was referring to as the third component of the tree of the three roots, was perhaps ahead of the conception later expressed by Mao. Zamora explained that the straw hat represented the people of Venezuela, and the military *kepi* signified that the army should be united with the people in order to achieve the federal revolution that was demanded in Venezuela.

Ezequiel Zamora seized the Bolivarian project. Unfortunately, he died at the beginning of the federal war. With him was buried the dream of the poor peasants of Venezuela, who were betrayed after the war of independence.

This aspect of our work, of course, certainly has its complement in all of Latin America. Because we are Venezuelans, we surely have taken three Venezuelans as roots for our ideological project, determined to resist the thesis that comes from the North. Someone told me recently that everything bad comes from the North: the thesis of the end of history, of the last man, of the technetronic era, the thesis that ideologies are no longer useful, that they are outdated. No. We resist. We do not accept these formulations. We have chosen these three symbolic figures instead.

A Panamanian captain, still in hiding four months ago, told me, "I am in hiding, Comandante, because I hanged a gringo and I have an arrest warrant for murder." (Now, where are the arrest warrants for the thousands of deaths caused by the invasion of

Panama?) He said to me, "Comandante, you have your god there, Bolívar; and we have our saint, Omar Torrijos."

In this way Martí is present in all the Americas. More recently, Omar Torrijos. More recently Juan Velasco Alvarado, a symbol of the soldier of the people in Peru and the immense experience of the Inca plan, or in the Southern Cone. One early morning, a few months ago, I received a secret emissary from Montevideo with a letter from active officers of the Uruguayan army, who are called *artiguista* soldiers, with a gift on the political thought of Artigas.

San Martín, Sandino, Mariátegui, and so many other Latin Americans.... I take this opportunity to say that I also feel very honored to have met and embraced today Comandante Daniel Ortega of the Nicaraguan Revolution, who is here in Havana, as you know. Therein lie the roots of a project for a nation, a single nation of which we are all Latin Americans and Caribbeans.

Here is a first aspect of work that is well suited, my Comandante, to the coming centennial year of José Martí's death. To strengthen that ideological work, the pairing of Bolívar and Martí, as a way of raising the enthusiasm and pride of Latin Americans.

The other aspect of our work, for which we also need to strengthen the ties with the peoples of our America, is organizational work.

In prison, we received many documents on how the Cuban people organized themselves after the triumph of the Revolution. We are determined to organize an immense social movement in Venezuela: the Bolivarian Revolutionary Movement-200. Beyond that, we are calling for the creation of the Bolivarian National Front for this coming year. We are calling the students, the peasants, the indigenous people, the retired military (because unfortunately the military in the barracks in Venezuela are still muzzled, and the political system, or the Venezuelan politicians, intend to have forever a military that is mute, deaf, and blind in the face of the national tragedy), the military who are in the streets, the intellectuals, the workers, the fishermen, the dreamers, all, to form this great social front to face the challenge of the transformation of Venezuela.

In Venezuela, nobody knows what may happen at any moment. For example, we are entering an electoral year, 1995. In a year's time, in December, there will be another illegal and illegitimate electoral process in Venezuela, marked by an abstention rate – you will not believe it – of 90% on average. That is to say, 90% of Venezuelans do not go to the polls, do not believe in the messages of politicians, and do not believe in almost any political party.

This year we aspire, with the Bolivarian Movement and with the National Bolivarian Front, to polarize Venezuela. Those who are going to the electoral process (where there are also honest people that we respect, but it is an electoral process that we do not believe in) are one pole. The other pole that we are going to nourish, push, and reinforce is the demand in the streets, with the people, to call for elections for a National Constituent Assembly, to redefine the fundamental structures of the republic that have collapsed. The juridical bases, the political bases, the economic bases, even the moral bases of Venezuela are in ruins, and this is not going to be fixed with band-aids.

Bolívar said, "Political gangrene cannot be cured with palliatives," and in Venezuela there is absolute and total gangrene.

A few months ago someone asked me why we did not allow the democratic system – what they call democratic in Venezuela – to mature. Taking advantage of the fact that I have tasted some delicious mango sweets here in Havana, I gave him the example of the mango (which is lost in Venezuela because we do not know how to benefit from it). I told him a green mango ripens, but a rotten mango will never ripen. We must rescue the seed from the rotten mango and sow it so that a new plant is born. This is what is happening in Venezuela today. This system has no way to recover itself.

And what I am going to say (I am going to use again the expression of the people of my town, of the Venezuelan *llano*), I am not going to say it because I feel handsome and encouraged here. I have said it in Venezuela: I have said it at the Ateneo de Caracas, which you know very well. I have said it to the press, to television, to the few programs that give us a place. I said it once in front of the Government Palace after I was released from prison. We do not discard the use of arms in Venezuela. We continue to have – and the government's own surveys say so – more than 80 percent favorable opinion in the Venezuelan military, in the army, in the navy, in the air force, and even in the National Guard, which is a force that invented and reinforced this system (it is like the regime's praetorian guard, but there are also good people there), and in the uniformed police, in the internal political direction, in the political police.

We have a force there and we feed it. We take care of it, although the young men, of course, are persecuted everywhere. Today if a Venezuelan officer names Bolívar in a speech in the barracks, he is considered a suspicious officer.

Despite all this, we have a force and, in addition to all this, we count on a very high percentage of Venezuelans, especially, dear friends, those 60% of Venezuelans who live in critical poverty.

Incredible, but true. Two hundred billion dollars have vanished in Venezuela in 20 years. "Where are they?" President Castro asked me. They are in the foreign accounts of almost all who have been in power in Venezuela. Civilians and military personnel who have enriched themselves under the protection of power.

In that immense majority of Venezuelans, we have a tremendous positive impact. You will understand that having these two forces, we are ready to give our all for the necessary change in Venezuela. That is why we do not discard the option of using the weapons of the people that are in the barracks and to look for that path if this political system decides, as it seems to have decided, to screw itself again and look for the means to manipulate and deceive.

We are calling for a Constituent Assembly and next year we will push for this as a short-term strategic resource.

To conclude these words, this greeting, this passion that moves me tonight, the third aspect in which we are working is a long-term strategic project in which the Cubans have and would have much to contribute and to discuss with us. It is a project with a 20 to 40-year horizon: building a sovereign economic model. We do not want to continue being a colonial economy, a subsidiary economic model.

For example, Venezuela has immense energy resources. No Caribbean or Latin American country should be exporting fuel to Europe. If Latin America has, among them, Venezuela with immense energy resources, why should Venezuela continue exporting 2.5 million barrels of crude oil per day to developed countries? Just as 500 years ago they took the raw material, today should they continue to take it in the same way?

It is a project we have already launched to the Venezuelan world under the name of "Simón Bolívar National Project," but with our arms extended to the Latin American and Caribbean continent. In this regard, we have already contacted some study centers in Panama, Colombia, Ecuador, Uruguay, Argentina, Chile, and Cuba. A project in which it is not far-fetched to consider, from the political point of view: to build an association of Latin American States. Why not think of this, the original dream of our liberators? Why continue to be fragmented? In the political area, the pretense for this project, which is not ours nor is it original, goes as far as 200 years old at least.

So many positive experiences in the cultural arena, in the economic arena (in this war economy in which Cuba is concretely living), in the sports arena, in the arena of health, of attention to the people, of attention to humanity, the first object of the homeland, the subject of the homeland.

So in that third aspect, in this long-term transformative political project, we extend our hands to the experience of the men and women of Cuba who have spent years thinking and working for this continental project.

To conclude, for now, we cordially invite you to a meeting in Santa Marta.

We have called to convene in Santa Marta, Colombia, on December 17. There we hope to begin preparations. This would be the first preparatory meeting for the Second Amphictyonic Congress of Panama, which we aspire to hold in Panama in 1996, the 170th anniversary of that first Congress, which was sabotaged by the North Americans. And we aspire to a third Congress in 1999, when the US army must withdraw its last soldier from that Bolivarian land and the Panama Canal.

This would be a Congress, or a Permanent League, where we Latin Americans would discuss our tragedy, our destiny. As that great revolutionary, that great Uruguayan writer, Eduardo Galeano said, destiny cannot be a curse. It is a defiance.

For us, the coming century is the century of hope. It is our century. It is the century of the resurrection of the Bolivarian dream, of Martí's dream, of the Latin American dream.

Dear friends, you have honored me by sitting down tonight to listen to these ideas of a soldier, of a Latin American fully and forever devoted to the cause of the revolution of our America.

A great Bolivarian embrace to you all.

Transcending capitalism

Speech at the closing of the World Social Forum on January 30, 2005 – Porto Alegre, Brazil

What joy! What youth! What emotion is felt here in Gigantinho Stadium! A hug from my soul to each and every one, a deep hug from my heart to all of you men, women, girls and boys – from Brazil, from Latin America, from the Caribbean, from North America, from Asia, from Africa, from Europe, from here – gathering the cry of all of us who are here, dreaming and fighting for a better possible and necessary world. I ask that we send a thunderous greeting to the peoples of the earth, to the peoples who fight, to the peoples who dream like us and together with us.

We are broadcasting to Venezuela live and direct, we are also broadcasting to Central America, South America. I assure you, I bet anything that a guy named Fidel Castro is watching this in Cuba. I am completely sure. Fidel! How's it going? How are you? There are cameras. Well, I'm sure because he was calling since 3 p.m., "What time are you going to talk, what time are you going to talk." "It's going!" I told him. "Wait, we have an agenda here."

Well, greetings to all. How beautiful this land is. This morning we toured and we saw the sunrise over the immense land of Brazil. Viva Brazil!

We left Caracas around midnight and landed here around 7 a.m. The sun was already over the horizon, a bright sun and a blue sky in Porto Alegre, and then we went on the road. We traveled an hour and a half by road through the savanna, the valley, looking at the fields and the people until we reached the peasant settlement of the Landless Workers' Movement, there in Tapes. We stayed there until noon, sharing with all the peasant leaders, communities, family farms. How one learns along these paths, how one is filled with strength by these immensities. Then we returned to a lunch where there was a very interesting debate with a group of intellectuals: thinkers from Brazil, America and the world, dialoguing and interacting with the leaders of the Porto Alegre World Social Forum. Then a somewhat noisy press conference.

João Pedro [Stedile] told me in a corridor there in the hotel that traveling with me is like a whirlpool of things. How did you say it, João? That walking with me is more complicated than seizing land.

Well, and then here we are, at the Gigantinho. And you who are the giants here, the giants of this land and above all the young people. Greetings to the youth. Raise your hands, young people. Long live the youth!

Ernesto Guevara used to say "the present is one of struggle, the future belongs to us." The future belongs to you girls and boys. Let's go for it. The future is yours.

A young man toured our continent on a motorcycle and later arrived in Central America, and witnessed the invasion of the gringos in Guatemala in 1954. One of the many invasions, one of the many abuses that North American imperialism has unleashed on this continent.

We are inspired by Che Guevara. We are inspired by old guys, some of them civilians, others soldiers. Che was civic-military. Military old guys like my general Omar Torrijos, that nationalist and revolutionary President of Panama. My general Juan Velasco Alvarado, president of Peru, leader of the Inca plan and the Peruvian national revolution. Inspired by old guys like Luis Carlos Prestes, the knight of hope. Viva Prestes!

We are also inspired by the old women, like the one Bolívar infinitely loved and called the Liberator of the Liberator. She was beautiful, and she was beautifully revolutionary, my colonel Manuela Sáenz. The Liberator of the Liberator, combatant in the

Battle of Ayacucho 180 years ago. Manuela went there for her love of the country and the Revolution, and of Bolívar. Manuela was so patriotic and loved Bolívar so much that she left her husband and wrote him a letter: "I say goodbye to you, darling, I am going with this man, this hurricane."

She left. She went to war. She was a revolutionary. Long live women!

There is an old guy that has inspired us many years, a bearded man. Recently thinking he was 20 years old, he jumped headfirst and broke his knee into eight pieces. But now he has recovered, although he told me he actually turned out better. We are inspired by that old guy called Fidel Castro.

Abreu e Lima, Artigas, San Martín, O'Higgins, Emiliano Zapata, Pancho Villa, Augusto Cesar Sandino, Morazán, all of them inspire us. They knew how to assume a commitment. They knew how to assume a commitment. Now, from here, from my heart I understand them, because we have assumed that commitment of all of them. Túpac Amaru, Guicaipuro, all those old guys.

Now those old guys have come back. One of those old guys, while he was dying – they were murdering him, cutting him to pieces, for imperialism has always been bestial. There is no good imperialism or bad imperialism: All imperialism is aberrant, bestial, perverse.

They had this Indian tied up. A horse pulled him one way and another horse pulled him another way, until his arms and his legs fell off. When he felt that he was already dying he shouted at the imperialists who were killing him, "*Today I die but someday I will return, made millions.*" Atahualpa has returned, made millions. Túpac Amaru has returned, made millions. Bolívar has returned, made millions. Sucre has returned, and Zapata, made millions.

And here we are. They have come back to us.

Well now, in this crowded place, Gigantinho, I also wanted first to thank you for the invitation you have given me. Second, to also say why I am here. I am here because, as I said two years ago right here in Porto Alegre, in the third edition of the World Social Forum, that this World Social Forum is the most important political event that occurs in the world every year. There is no other of this magnitude.

I am here because, together with my colleagues and comrades from the Venezuelan delegation, we come to learn, to imbue ourselves with more passion, more love, and more knowledge. I am here because this World Social Forum in Porto Alegre, in these five years, has become a solid platform for debate and discussion. A solid, wide, varied, rich platform, where most of the excluded, those who do not have a voice in the spaces of power, come to express themselves. To voice their protest. They come here to sing. They come to say what they are and what they want. They come here to express their poems, their songs, their hope, to seek consensus. I am here for these things and for many more. I am also here to thank, on behalf of the Venezuelan people, all the gestures of support, of solidarity that from this space and many others represented here have always reached Venezuela. The Bolivarian Venezuela that has been attacked by imperialism in recent years. I am here to give thanks on behalf of our people.

And on the other hand, comrades, how is it that I am here? Believe me, I do not feel like a president here at all. I am not here as a president. The president thing is just a circumstance. I am Hugo, I am not the president. Circumstantially, I am fulfilling my role like any role in a team, like the goalkeeper, the forward, the pitcher, or the catcher. Or the soldier who is in the vanguard, or the one who is in the rear. Or the worker who is plowing the land, or the one who is fertilizing the land, or the one who draw in the harvest. In short, I occupy a role, but I am a peasant, I am a soldier, I am a man committed to this alternative project of a better and possible world that is necessary to save the earth.

In this way, I come to Porto Alegre: as one more militant. A militant of the revolutionary cause, because I am a revolutionary. Every day I am more revolutionary because every day I am more convinced that the only path through which we can break the capitalist hegemony and the hegemony of the oligarchies of these lands, is the path of revolution. There is no other way.

Yesterday we were busy in Caracas attending to a very important visit by the Vice President of the People's Republic of China, along with a high-level delegation, and we signed 19 agreements between us. I said that relations between the Bolivarian Revolution and the Chinese Revolution are already projected from the subsoil to the stratosphere. We are already exploring together to look for oil and gas in Venezuela. We have also signed an agreement to build a satellite in China, which we will launch from China, but it will be a Venezuelan satellite. Venezuela will finally have its satellite. So our relations go from the subsoil to the stratosphere. Now I beg your maximum attention to what I want to say: the Chinese vice president brought me a gift. I have been a Maoist, since I was a boy, since I entered the Academy Military when I began to read Mao Zedong's military writings, philosophical writings, political theses, and *Red Book*. I began to read Che's *El Libro Verde Olivo*, Bolívar's speeches and letters. In short, I became a Maoist, a Bolivarian, a mixture of all that, and so the vice president brought me the collection of the complete writings of Mao Zedong, the Great Helmsman.

So I came by plane rereading the first volume. In the first volume and in the first chapter, Mao Zedong confronts a theme that is vital for every revolution and for every revolutionary: "It is essential," he said, "to clearly specify who are the friends and who are the enemies." He says that all the revolutions in Chinese history failed. They failed because, among other fundamental things, the revolutionaries were sometimes agitated by the passions of the moment and of the contradictions that were occurring everywhere freely, but there were also people who were in charge of accentuating them from the inside and from the outside.

On many occasions, we lose sight of our true friends and our true enemies. It is important that in Latin America, we clearly specify who are the true friends, and who are the true enemies.

In short, I am convinced that only through the path of the revolution will we be able to emerge from the position in which we have been for centuries. 500 years. 200 years. Here in Rio Grande do Sul, the great river of the South, one can also name the great lands of the South, the great valleys of the South, the great seas of the South, the great dreams of the South.

The South also exists. Now, with all due respect to you northerners; there are many people here from North America. There are also revolutionaries in North America, of course, and many revolutionaries in the North, in Europe. But I really think that there is more awareness about the need for urgent, rapid, and profound changes in the South of the world. They have woken up again in the northern world. However, where there is greater awareness, where greater force has been unleashed, is in the South. The South has endured for centuries the abuses of the North. The abuses are not of the peoples of the North, but of the empires of the North.

Being here in the South also reminds me, comrades, that in April of this year, it will be 50 years since a very important event took place in Indonesia in 1955: the Bandung Summit, from which the Movement of the Non-Aligned was born. That is good to remember because it has been barely half a century. 200 years ago, Simón Bolívar convened the summit of Panama in 1826. Next year we will have to commemorate the 180th anniversary of the Amphictyonic Congress of Panama, which was swept away by the North American empire.

Simón Bolívar was, if not the first, one of the first anti-imperialists on this earth. Simón Bolívar came to foresee the imperialist threat from North America. Simón Bolívar even wrote in a letter, in 1828: "The United States of America seems destined by providence to plague America with misery in the name of freedom." It was written in his own handwriting in 1828.

But the Indonesian summit of 1955, the summit called by Tito, by Nehru, and by Sukarno, was a summit to call for the unity of the countries and peoples of Asia and Africa. From there arose the Non-Aligned Movement. From there arose the conscience of the South. From there arose the South Commission directed by the great African leader, Julius Nyerere.

Nyerere died very recently, in the 1990s. Nyerere died, and the South Commission was re-appointed, and proposals began to be made. But then the collapse of the Soviet Union and the fall of the Berlin Wall occurred. And as Joseph Stiglitz says, then came the happy 90s: the end of history, the last man, the technetronic era. The consciousness of the South fell into the depths of the Antarctic ice, and the proposal of Washington hit us like an avalanche: neocolonialism dressed up as a thesis, misleading some, and all those policies of the International Monetary Fund, injected in overdose quantities, especially to the countries of Latin America.

Today from Rio Grande do Sul in the World Social Forum, there is no more appropriate space to say it: to save the world we need many things. One of the first is relaunching the awareness of the South. I even say more comrades: It is possible that some in the North do not realize it, but the future of the North depends on the South.

Because if we do not do what we have to do, if we don't really make that other, better world possible, and if we fail, the world will be pushed behind the bayonets of the North American Marines, behind the murderous bombs of Mr. Bush. If there were not the necessary strength, awareness, and organization in the South to resist the attacks of neo-imperialism and the Bush doctrine, it would prevail in the world. The world would go straight to destruction. In how many years, I don't know. There are some scientific reports that say that if the planet continues to overheat at the rate that it has been overheating, in 100 years the temperature of the planet will have produced a strong thaw in the polar ice caps. The terrible tsunami that hit the coast of Asia a week ago and caused 200-odd thousand deaths would fall short of the giant ocean waves that would destroy entire towns, and submerge countries would remain under their waters. If the ozone layer continues to break into pieces and the sun continues inclemently hitting the earth's crust, fires, temperatures, and universal suffocation would end a good part of the life on the planet. This is just to focus on the geographical, physical, and natural point of view, because it is possible that long before the thaw occurs the planet would be set on fire by violent rebellions. The peoples are not going to settle in peace to the imposition of a model like neoliberalism, like colonialism.

An indigenous leader on this continent said it well a few years ago after a rebellion when the indigenous took up arms and went to the mountains, and a journalist asked him: Why did you do this? What moved you to take up arms? And he answered very clearly: "Because I'd rather die fighting than starve."

A year ago we began to launch this idea of the need to retake the consciousness, the spaces, and the proposals of the South. I asked myself yesterday in Caracas and on the plane last night and this morning, what should be my central objective? Essentially, what have I come for?

Of course, I could start by saying that I come here to express in a few words what has been happening in Venezuela since my last visit to Porto Alegre in January 2003, when we were still in full battle against the imperialist forces that were attacking Venezuela. The Venezuelan oil industry was still nearly paralyzed then. They sabotaged our refineries, they sabotaged our ships, oil wells, electrical systems, and computer systems. They tried to force the Venezuelan people to surrender due to hunger. They tried to implode the country so that the government would leave and the president would resign. After the military coup, after terrorism, after the imperialist aggression, after the oil economic aggression, and the capital flight, I remember that when I went to Porto Alegre in January 2003, we were making the decision on currency exchange control. We had suspended the sale of dollars for two weeks in order to establish a rigid exchange control system. In Venezuela, there will continue to be exchange control over the Venezuelan currency, to protect the country from financial speculation, from the engulfing capital that has taken over many countries.

As a result of the exchange control, international reserves have already broken records, and we are close to 25 billion dollars, but on that occasion, we were still in full battle. Nothing clearly indicated that we were going to win the battle, but we had much faith that we were going to achieve it, because of the response of the people, the response of the Armed Forces, and the response of the oil workers who took the oil industry on their shoulders and allowed us to recover it; to the people who took over the refineries, the oil fields, and the gasoline transporters and moved them to the same town together with the soldiers, demonstrating to the Venezuelan oligarchy that the Venezuelan people do not give up and will never give up.

So many things have happened in these two years. So many things have happened that allow me to reflect with you on the truth of that expression by Leon Trotsky, when he said that every revolution from time to time needs the whip of the counterrevolution. The counterrevolution whipped us. The Yankees whipped us with economic sabotage, media sabotage, social sabotage, terrorism, bombs, violence, blood and death, *coup d'état*, manipulation of institutions, and international pressure. They intended to convert Venezuela into a country guided by the Organization of American States and to install a special consul in Venezuela, who gave a press conference every day, trying to establish a supranational power above our laws, above our institutions, above our Constitution. We resisted all of this.

That counterrevolutionary attack allowed us first to defend ourselves, resisting the aggression, resisting, resisting, and resisting until we had to move to the counterattack. That was how in 2003, Venezuela recovered its oil industry from the hands of the Venezuelan oligarchy and the North American empire. We recovered the oil industry, but that was a battle, a real economic, social, communicational, technological, popular, and even military war. Those were the days of Plaza Altamira and the calls for military rebellion and for US military intervention. To give an example, comrades, of how the revolutionary government is now, how the revolution has been strengthened, thanks to the counterrevolutionary attack and the revolutionary counter-offensive, I give you this data: Last year, 2004, we distributed from Venezuela's own oil budget, not from the national budget, almost 4 billion dollars to social investment, to education, to health, to microcredit, to housing, above all, to the poorest, as Victor Hugo would say, to the miserable. Of course, the neoliberals would say that this is throwing away money. Chávez is throwing out money, they would say, but they gave it to the gringos and distributed it among their profitable businesses. We have implemented an extraordinary system, for example, of scholarships. Almost everyone is studying: grandmothers, grandfathers, children, and grandchildren.

Those who did not finish primary school or secondary school are finishing it; there are men and women of 50, 40, 20, 80, 90, studying with a television and some videos, using the Cuban method. All the videos were edited in Cuba, thanks to the support of the Cuban Revolution, and thanks to the participation of the Venezuelan people. One day I found a classmate of mine from high school. We graduated together from fifth year. I went to the Military Academy, and he got married and could not continue studying. He already has grandchildren, and I saw him in a classroom studying. Initially, I didn't recognize him, but he told me, "Hugo, don't you remember me?" After I remembered who he was, he told me, "I could never go to university, but 30 years later, Hugo, here I am. I want to study mathematics," he told me, "after 30 years."

Or a grandmother who learned to read and write. And she does not stop there, now she goes to primary school and then she will go to secondary school. In a speech she gave in front of many people in Caracas when she received her degree she said, "I couldn't help my children study because I didn't know how to read or write, but now I'm helping my grandchildren study, I help them do their homework." 99% of these people are poor or very poor, many of them live in misery, so we devised a system of scholarships, and today we are giving out half a million scholarships. Each scholarship is at 100 dollars a month, so that's 50 million dollars a month, almost 600 million dollars a year, just in scholarships. Ah! The neoliberals say that this is throwing money away. No! That money used to be stolen. Now we are redistributing it: giving power to the poor, so that they can defeat their poverty.

Just another example of everything that has been happening as part of this revolutionary counter-offensive: in 2003, in response to imperialist aggression, the missions emerged and today we have the Barrio Adentro Mission underway. The Barrio Adentro Mission is a medical mission, also supported by revolutionary Cuba. Today in Venezuela there are almost twenty thousand Cuban doctors and Cuban dentists living with the poorest people alongside Venezuelan nurses and health committees in the neighborhoods. Most of the budget of the Barrio Adentro Mission goes to pay the costs of medicines. Not a penny is charged to the people to support the doctors, the transport systems, communication, the construction of outpatient clinics, the consultations, the equipment, or the team. All that, most of that budget, comes from the oil income that used to go abroad. The transnationals and the Venezuelan oligarchy took advantage of the oil wealth that never returned to the Venezuelan people.

The Barrio Adentro Mission is now spread throughout the country. In 2004, the Barrio Adentro Mission attended to more than 50 million cases with totally free consultations, free medication included. Keep in mind that Venezuela is not Brazil, and that in Venezuela we are barely 26 million inhabitants. That is, the Barrio Adentro Mission in one year gave consultations or saw cases equivalent to twice the Venezuelan population. That figure is higher than all the medical and dental consultations that were given in Venezuela in all hospitals, and in all outpatient clinics in the last five years.

You see, this is an example of the revolution in Venezuela. Those boys are from the Bolivarian University, a university that is barely a year old. Thank you, keep going, keep going as long as the future is yours.

The revolution, among many other things, is an acceleration of processes. Acceleration and deepening, above all, toward a society of equals, in which no one is excluded. Most of these boys had been waiting years for admission to a university. They could not enter the universities. The universities were privatized. That is the neoliberal imperialist plan. Health had been privatized, but cannot be privatized, it is a fundamental human right. Health, education, water, electricity, public services, they cannot be handed over to the voracity of private capital. That denies the rights of the peoples. That is the path to savagery. Capitalism is savagery. Every day, I am more convinced of this. I have not the slightest doubt. It is necessary, we say (along with many intellectuals of the world), to transcend capitalism. But I add, capitalism is not going to transcend within capitalism itself. No. Capitalism must be transcended by way of socialism. This is the way to go beyond the capitalist model. True socialism. Equality! Justice!

As Ignacio Ramonet said, it is possible. It is possible to transcend capitalism by way of socialism and beyond in democracy. In democracy! But watch out and listen to the beat. In what kind of democracy? It is not the democracy that Mr. Superman wants to impose on us from Washington. No, that is not democracy.

By the way, recently Condoleezza, 'Condolences,' rather, 'Condolences Rice' said, "look where imperialism is coming from now." Where does imperialism come from? They know that inside Venezuela they have no strength. Even if they invaded us, we would make them bite the dust of defeat there on the Caribbean coast, and in the waters of the Orinoco, and the heroic savannas of Venezuela where the centaurs of Bolívar and Abreu E Lima rode. Liberators of these lands, the heroic people of Venezuela, the same as that of Brazil and all the peoples of this America of ours.

When these peoples decide for freedom, there is no force capable of stopping them.

I admire Che a lot and I sing to him, and read him, and remember him. But Che's thesis was unfeasible at that time. The *foco guerillero*, 100 men on a mountain, could have been valid as it was in Cuba, but the conditions were very different, and that is why Che died in Bolivia, died like a Quixote, and he himself said: "I feel under my legs the ribs of Rocinante," saying goodbye to his parents, saying goodbye to his children. One of Che's daughters, Aleida Guevara, she's here somewhere, this morning I saw her covered in dirt over there, following her in father's ways. Viva Che Guevara!

Today the situation is different. It is no longer the conditions of the *foco guerillero*, which can be surrounded by rangers or marines on a mountain, like they surrounded Che, and massacred them one by one. Of course then it was a squad of 50 men against 500, with very old weapons, not like now. Now we are millions. How are they going to surround us, where are they going to surround us?

Be careful, they might be the ones who end up surrounded!

Be careful – if one day that happens and you are surrounded, surrender. There are so many of us that we could surround them, no, not yet, little by little, not yet. No, not all empires can be surrounded, they are empires, they rot from the inside.

All empires rot from the inside, and the day comes when they fall, and they are left in pieces like the Roman empire and all the empires of Europe and of past centuries. One day the rot that North American imperialism carries inside will finish tearing it down, and the great people of Martin Luther King will be freed.

To the great North American people, who are our brother people, I send my greetings and our greetings to the people of the United States of America, to the people of Canada, to the peoples of Europe and to all the peoples of the world.

Now, on top of what occurred in Venezuela in 1993 and what has allowed us to strengthen ourselves, in the social, economic, political, national, and international arenas, today Venezuela is stronger than ever before in the last 100 years. Inwardly and outwardly, facing the whole world, it is a strengthened homeland, it is a strengthened people, it is a strengthened and strengthening revolution.

We are not singing victory. Only recognizing that reality indicates the process, and we must take care of it every day. It is one of my proclamations, always to my colleagues, to my colleagues: every day. Che used to say that the revolution cannot be fought with efficiency, we need revolutionary efficiency. To be more effective, and more efficient every day, to fight against old vices such as corruption, lack of values, which are threats that are always on the loose. Inefficiency and corruption, two great threats, bureaucratism. Che also said the fight against bureaucratism is a daily struggle for every revolutionary, so that we are not chained by bureaucracy, or rather, bureaucratism.

In 2004, it was a great victory, a great political victory, when we went to the recall referendum. They said that I was doing everything possible to avoid it, because they didn't want to tell me, as the neoliberals say, that they were afraid of the people – lies! I never did anything to prevent it, only insisted that they complied with the constitutional requirements. They had to collect the signatures within the established period, they had to do what the institutions say. And it was not the OAS [Organization of American States] or the North American government that was going to present the signatures. They had to collect them in the street. At the end they collected them, even though there were many doubts, hundreds of thousands of repeated false signatures, and signatures of people who died a long time ago.

However, in the end the Electoral Council said yes, that there was the required amount of 20%, and so I was the first to say, let's to the referendum. I told them we are going to defeat them, and we defeated them on August 15 with 60% of the votes, much more than five years ago.

Then in the regional elections of October 31 for the 24 governorships we won 22, and the two that we did not win we lost by a fluke. 22 governorships, more than 80% of the mayors, more than 80% of the regional deputies, that is an advance.

In the social sphere, in the social model of inclusion, for an advance in the political sphere, another very important thing is the strengthening of the judiciary. In Venezuela there was a *coup d'état*. They arrested me, they took me, kidnapped, to an island and later the judges of the Supreme Court said that there had been no coup, that I was guarded by soldiers full of good intentions, and that what had happened was a vacuum of power; Washington's thesis. No longer; now the Judicial Power, the Citizen Power, has been strengthened.

The National Assembly couldn't even legislate because of the sabotage. On one occasion the revolutionary deputies had to go to session outside the Legislative Palace. But by the end of 2004, especially in the end, they ended up approving fundamental laws such as the Law on Social Responsibility on Radio and Television, and many other laws, like the Organic Law of the Supreme Court of Justice, which now allows us to clean up the judiciary. The slowness of some processes is one of the difficulties of democratic revolutions.

I insist and emphasize that no one despair. Simón Bolívar said it very clearly, and I bring his voice here to repeat it. If we want to have a country, let us have patience and more patience, perseverance and more perseverance, work and more work. Let no one despair!

With patience, perseverance and a lot of work, a lot of awareness, the changes are happening. Of course they are not going to happen by themselves, they have to be promoted.

In the end of 2003-04, we experienced economic strengthening. The growth of the Venezuelan economy last year was 20% and unemployment fell. It had gone from more than 20%, it fell to 11%. Inflation, product of economic sabotage, had risen more than 30 years and is now close to 20% again. It is still very high, but it has been dropping substantially. International reserves have broken historical records, oil production has fully recovered, we are producing more than three million barrels of oil per day.

In short, the economy is growing. Manufacturing, agriculture – for example, for the first time in a long time Venezuela can say that it does not have to import rice. We are self-sufficient in rice, in corn, and we will continue to recover agriculture now with the war against the latifundio. We recognize the example of the Landless Workers' Movement, who have been an example for us, and an example for all the peasants of this continent, of the struggle for land, for justice in the countryside and for food sovereignty.

I will leave it here regarding the progress of the revolution in the social, political, economic, national, and international spheres. Venezuela entered Mercosur in 2004. The South American community of nations was born, even though I have been critical of the profile that was initially given to it. But though critical we are all there, because just as some criticized me five years ago for attending the Summit of the Americas in Canada, in the end I was the only president present who opposed the FTAA [Free Trade Area of the Americas] project.

In that year 2000, and since then, we began our anti-FTAA campaign, because the FTAA is nothing more than a colonialist project. Look, we cannot say that we have won. We are far from the objective, from the goal of creating an alternative integration model that we call the Bolivarian Alternative for Latin America, the ALBA, that is walking, advancing. One would like it to be faster, but there is reality. The sun rose on January 1, 2005 and ALBA went to hell.

Where is ALBA, mister? ALBA is dead, ALBA does not exist. What exists out there are *"Albitas"* but still North American imperialism did not have strength, despite so much blackmail and so much pressure to impose the neocolonial model on the peoples of this continent.

Now, I don't want to overestimate the empire's weaknesses. It would be fatal to underestimate the adversary. Nevertheless, we must objectively recognize the weaknesses of the adversary, because if one believes that the adversary is invincible, then he is invincible. North American imperialism is not invincible. It is not invincible. There is Vietnam in history. There are the people of Iraq resisting the outrage of the invasion. There is revolutionary Cuba, 40 years resisting US imperialism. There is Bolivarian Venezuela resisting US imperialism for six years. The empire is not invincible.

That is important to know, do you know why? Because there are people who in good faith think that it is invincible, and that they cannot strike imperialism even with a rose petal, that they cannot even say anything because it can get upset, it can get angry. Well, on one occasion when I was going to Baghdad, we were in Tehran and from Tehran we were going to go to Baghdad, it was around 1990 – Ali, the press spokesman went out saying in Washington: Chávez should not go to Baghdad and that they were very irritated. Then some journalists asked me: Look, what do you think that those are irritated, and I said: Well, if they are irritated, I am going to send them a gigantic shipment of Coppertone. I don't give a damn if they're angry in Washington!

What does it matter to me? Simón Bolívar said it in 1811 in Caracas, when some fearful and novices refused to declare independence from the Spanish empire. Simón Bolívar launched an incendiary speech. That 27-year-old boy said: *"And what does it matter to us that Spain sells Bonaparte his slaves if we are willing to be free,"* or as General San Martí said, the great liberator of the South, *"Let us be free, nothing else matters."* What we are is free and we want to be definitely free, whatever the cost, whatever happens.

Goliath is not invincible; imperialism is not invincible. Ah! That makes it more dangerous, if it is true, because as imperialism begins to feel its weaknesses then it begins to resort to brutal force. The attack against Venezuela using brute force is a sign of ideological weakness, which is one of the greatest weaknesses. Hardly anyone dares to defend neoliberalism anymore. Just three years ago Fidel and I were almost alone in those meetings of presidents. It was like a neoliberal choir and one felt like an infiltrator there, conspiring. Today almost no one dares to defend the neoliberal model. That is one of weaknesses. Neoliberalism has been stripped bare. The ideological weaknesses are evident, even the economic weaknesses are evident, and these weaknesses all indicate that they will continue to increase.

Just look at the internal repression in the United States, the so-called Patriot Act. What is it if not a repressive law against US citizens? They talk about freedom of expression and violate it every day. They have a group of imprisoned journalists prosecuted because they did not reveal their sources of information. They persecute journalists, they do not allow photos to be taken of the corpses of US soldiers, many of them Latino, by the way, who return from Iraq. No one can take photos of them. They bury them there in secret. Those are signs of Goliath's weakness.

On the other hand, it is necessary to recognize old and new actors that arise on the geopolitical map, and that also influence the strengths and weaknesses of North American imperialist hegemony. I am no longer talking about the internal weaknesses of imperialism, objectively or subjectively. Russia, for example, is rising. It is no longer Russia kneeling to Washington's mandates. There is a new Russian nationalism. I have seen it, I have felt it in the streets of Moscow.

Until a few years ago hardly anyone dared to speak of Karl Marx in Moscow. Hardly anyone dared to speak of Vladimir Ilyich Ulyanov in Moscow, or in the villages of Russia. Russia has risen. It is no longer the kneeling Russia that inspired sadness and pity. There is a good president at the helm, Vladimir Putin. And China is advancing, growing, becoming stronger. China is already a world power. Economically China has been growing for 20 years at an average rate of 19 percent, experiencing technological growth, autonomy, and food sovereignty. There is a united Europe, and now with a new socialist government in Spain, it is no longer the government of Aznar kneeling also to the mandates of imperialism. In Africa. I recently visited that other guy called Muammar El Gaddafi; we were there in Tripoli talking for a while with Ahmed Ben Bella, that Algerian and African leader, one of those Arab peoples who have been battling for centuries for their beliefs, with their gods, with their dreams. Gaddafi told me that he sees the process of African unity with great optimism. The president of Algeria, his good friend Abdelaziz Bouteflika, tells me the same thing. Iran is strengthened. In November I was with President Mohammed Khatami and with the leader Khomeini. Iran is strengthened. The Americans wanted Iran to suspend its nuclear research. Iran resisted and in the end the Iranians' thesis prevailed. US imperialism could not beat them and did not get the support of the United Nations, nor the support of Europe. And Latin America today is not the same Latin America as it was five years ago. The first two years of my government, many of my supporters criticized me; they asked me to go faster, they asked me to be more radical. I thought that it was not the moment, and it was not the moment because there are phases in the processes, comrades.

There are phases and there are rhythms, which have to do not only with the internal situations of each country but with the international situation. Even risking that some of you make noises of disapproval, I don't care, I love Lula. Lula is a good man, with a big heart. He is a brother and a comrade. I give him my embrace, my affection as a brother, as a comrade. And I am sure that with Lula and with the people of Brazil, with Néstor Kirchner and the Argentine people, with Tabaré Vázquez and the Uruguayan people, we will pave the way toward the dream of a united Latin America. An embrace to all of you. I love you very much everyone, thank you very much.

This is called socialism

Speech at the Inauguration Ceremony on January 10, 2007 – Caracas, Venezuela

EVERYONE, ALL THE PEOPLE of Venezuela; The excellent and very well-structured speech given by Cilia Flores, President of the National Assembly, will allow me to save a few minutes in my words on this special day of January 10, 2007. I thank the President for reminding us of those clear and sharp traces of our most recent history, taking as inspiration the deepest roots of *venezolanidad*, of Venezuelan indigeneity, of Venezuelan spirituality, of the depths of our *venezolanidad*.

The President of the National Assembly reminded us precisely of where we come from. It is always fundamental, friends, deputies, compatriots, it is always important – more than important – to have a knowledge of history, and to not forget where we come from, our roots, and the causes that generated the events that brought all of us here. It is essential, and that is why it was said that since the beginning of 1989, the last decade of the 20th century was an earth-shaking and earth-shattering decade. The eruption of those restrained forces, oppressed for so long; the moral, ethical, and spiritual forces of a repressed people, as Cilia said, exploded that February 27th in these same streets, in this same valley, and then on February 4th, 1992, and on November 4th, 1992. Three political earthquakes signaled the end of an era. They were announcing the end of an era and the advent of a new era, of a new epoch. That is where we come from.

As Antonio Gramsci explains it, it is a historical crisis when

This is called socialism

something is dying and does not finish dying, and at the same time, something is being born and does not finish being born. We come from the eye of the hurricane of this historical crisis. Moreover, it should be said, we are now in the eye of the hurricane of that historical crisis, and we will be all our lives. All our lives will be marked by the eye of a hurricane, beyond which are undoubtedly the horizons of the new Homeland. Bolívar in Angostura – I am going to allow myself to read some of the bolts of lightning Bolívar launched that February 15 in the Orinoco, so that we can see and feel once again not only how valid this concept is, but also just how alive, and how it is in the heart of today's Venezuela and in the essence of the Bolivarian project, which is why it is named "Bolivarian."

I read: "My opinion is, legislators, that the foundation of our system depends immediately and exclusively on the equality established and practiced in Venezuela..." This is called socialism. Equality is impossible in capitalism; it is only possible in socialism. That is why, without exaggeration of any kind, I have been affirming that the philosophy of Simón Bolívar is true socialist philosophy. Bolívar, as we know, was a master of words. He took great care of words and used them with great precision. Therefore he says here: "Our system, the foundation of our system, depends immediately..." Bolívar specifies a time. It is essential to assign time to a project, and what is more, Bolívar also sets the time to zero, if we were to use mathematics. Time at zero: "the foundation of our system depends immediately and exclusively..." He also gives it space. He places it in the heart, in the essence of the foundations of the system that was being created to escape the 300 years of colonialism. The system of established and practiced equality is not only declared. Established and practiced makes it eternal, and therefore, permanent in thought.

We are in the age that Bolívar and his dream referred to. We are in the next age, in the bicentennial. At the end he closes his speech: "Dignified legislators, deign to grant Venezuela an eminently popular government, eminently just, eminently moral; that chains oppression, anarchy, and guilt; a government that triumphs under the rule of the inexorable laws of equality and freedom." This provokes us to include it in the oath we take as governors, mayors, ministers, deputies, deputies, and president.

It could be a perfect text for a profound and Bolivarian oath: "I swear to grant Venezuela an eminently popular government, eminently just, eminently moral; that chains oppression, anarchy and guilt; a government that triumphs under the rule of inexorable laws."

Let us hear then, compatriots, the tremendous moral burden, the tremendous political burden, and even more the tremendous socialist burden of the philosophy and project of Simón Bolívar. A project that as we know was buried in Santa Marta, in Berruecos, in San Carlos de Cojedes on a day like today in 1860 when the Venezuelan oligarchy, taking cover in treason, managed to assassinate one of the greatest Bolivarians, one of the greatest Venezuelans, one of the greatest leaders that this people has birthed: my General Ezequiel Zamora. Viva Zamora!

I want to return to Bolívar's initial approach in that speech to which I was referring, which I find very orienting, which is why I wanted to bring forth several excerpts from that speech in Angostura.

The first thought I brought here today, the same thought I brought here eight years ago: "Blessed is the citizen who under the shield of the arms of his command summons the national sovereignty to exercise its absolute will." Absolute will!

Bolívar and his democratic-revolutionary approach, not democratic-bourgeois. He does not speak of elites; he attacks the elites. He always speaks of the people, of summoning the people.

Bolívar and his vision. Take note. A few years before Karl Marx, Bolívar indicates, conceptualizes, and places the people at the center of the activators of the machine of history. The popular masses are the fundamental actors of the historical process, not individuals, not particular persons. It is the masses; it is the people. That is a vision that Karl Marx developed a few years later: dialectical materialism. We must not fear this!

I have heard of some sectors of national life that seem to be frightened because we talk about socialism, but they should be frightened of talk of capitalism.

I would like to recall that in my speech on February 2, 1999, I made an analysis from my modest point of view of what I called Venezuela's catastrophic crisis: the crisis that developed and became a general catastrophe, particularly in the last part of the 20th century. A moral, economic, social, political, and military crisis that degenerated, or evolved, into a catastrophe. That ended – well, it did not end – it expressed itself like a volcano on February 27, 1989.

From the juridical-political perspective, what occurred on February 27 was the explosion of constituent power, a concept that as we know has been circulating throughout the world and is sometimes manipulated, misunderstood, and little known since the days of the French Revolution. The thesis of constituent power that originates from the people emerged with force in the French Revolution. Bolívar touched this. He saw up close the impacts of that Revolution, particularly in the last period when Napoleon said: *"La Revolución c'est fini…"* The Revolution ended. Bolívar witnessed these events. [Francisco de] Miranda lived them and brought that experience here to the First Republic.

So then, in 1998 and 1999 we invoked the constituent power, as we had been doing since before, developing the concept, and evaluating what happened in 1989 and in 1992, giving, or trying to give direction to the uncontrollable events that were unleashed. That is how we raised the flags of the original, plenipotentiary constituent power. That is how constituent power should be.

Three thousand days later, I invoke again the original, omnipresent, plenipotentiary constituent power. I summon it again, today, January 10, 2007. The constituent power has always existed, because in decisive moments it becomes a fundamental actor and imposes its strengths, converting potential into power like a giant engine or a million giant engines. What was it that happened on April 13? What emerged? What was activated? It alone. No one summoned it; it was summoned. It had to sweep away fascism, sweep away imperialism, and defend its decision, its sovereignty.

In a given moment, that is to say, in a certain time and space, the constituent power is activated. Someone starts engines, sometimes without prior planning, sometimes with prior planning. What happened on August 15, 2004? A referendum. The constituent power once again took to the streets to impose its strength, converting the potential into a transforming force so that the Revolution would not end. And what happened on December 3, 2006? Those seven and a half million votes, those millions and millions of souls, hearts and wills were nothing else but the constituent power converted into a fundamental actor of its own history in just one day. I invoke and summon the original constituent power of the Venezuelan people to continue, to speed up, to accelerate.

I am willing, and I ask all of us to do so. Starting today, we are going to transform 2007 into a stage of permanent and growing galvanization. This is what I have been thinking during these days of December, and the first days of January: How to create a group of what I am considering calling "constituent engines." All this has to do with the long-term perspective of the Bolivarian Revolution. Let us not forget that we have also said that December 3 was a point not of arrival but of departure, a starting point for a new era into which we have already entered. More than just decreeing it, more than just saying it, we have to transform it into a daily reality, a permanent reality, an accelerated reality. This is how I see it and this is how I feel it.

We have closed a cycle. It is not easy to do this with such a short distance of time for analysis, it is not easy at all. I understand

and accept that I am venturing, but I believe it is necessary to venture in the analysis, to accelerate the times. Simón Bolívar said: "Revolutions must be seen from close and evaluated from afar." In this case, I am not evaluating it. I am seeing it; We are seeing it.

But just like a galloping horse, one must try to hold the reins and regulate the pace. That is why I say, I see, feel, and believe that we have closed a cycle now in December 2006, or we could say today, more precisely today, January 10, 2007. Today a cycle is coming to an end. What we may well call a transition period is coming to an end. Let us ask ourselves and let us see the situation the country is experiencing today and that which the country was experiencing eight years ago, three thousand days ago.

I already said this a short while ago. So many things have happened, so many things! Well, they have changed even though there is still a threat, there are still debts, and there are still wrinkles that run throughout, but it is a transition. Not only is a new era beginning; we are fully entering into the period of construction of the Simón Bolívar National Project, which required a solid foundation.

What we have done so far is to lay a floor on which we will build the edifice, the Bolivarian Socialist Project that is only just beginning. From there, how do we make the leap, how do we achieve the end of one period and the start of another? From there, reflecting, I believe that we can achieve it, among many other things, with this battery – that is what I call it – this set of constituent engines, like machines. We know the engine is a machine made to extract energy from the creative power of the multitude.

Let us put the people there, they are the wise, they are the owners, they are the sovereign. Let us put them again in the first stage as constituent engines to finish breaking the old system and give life to the new system. The constituent power, as another space, as another time, an acceleration of time; that is one of the characteristics of the constituent power. It allows us to activate, even to change historical time. Everything is relative, as has been demonstrated, Einstein demonstrated it.

By the way, I received an article by Héctor Navarro on the reflections of Einstein called "Why socialism?" I recommend reading this article. A wise man, a genius, he concluded that the only possible path is socialism. But time, as we know, is relative, space is also relative, everything is relative. The constituent power allows us to relativize, to break with modernizing rationalism and to open new spaces and new times. That is why it is essential that we activate and summon it.

By accelerating time and giving a new dynamic to space, as Toni [Antonio] Negri says in a good book that Juan Barreto gave me: Constituent power breaks the category of the modern, the rationalism of the modern that pretends to freeze time and freeze space behind the death mask of rationalism. It is necessary to break that old paradigm.

What are these engines? I already spoke a bit about the five constituent engines the day before yesterday at the swearing-in ceremony of the new Cabinet. I ask the National Assembly, the Powers of the State, the Republican moral power, the Electoral Power, the Judicial Power, the Ombudsman's Office, the regional powers – governors, mayors, municipal councils, parish councils – I ask that we make a sustained and united, a unified effort in this direction.

The first of the five constituent engines I am referring to is a law of laws. The President of the Assembly has already announced, and I am very grateful to all the deputies for approving my request, that this law will become one of the constituent engines, a revolutionary law of laws, the mother of laws: the Enabling Law. In a few days, or rather hours, Madam President, we will be submitting the request to this worthy Assembly. A Revolutionary Law of Laws.

To give you an example, notice the Venezuelan Code of Commerce, which is a symbol of capitalism. We still have a Code of Commerce drafted more than 100 years ago in 1904, and several

This is called socialism

reforms were made to that Code, but within the same framework. The last one was made in 1955 when General Marcos Pérez Jímenez ruled Venezuela. That is the Code of Commerce. What socialism will we build with a Code of Commerce of that kind, to say the least? To give just this one example, as far as the reform of a set of laws is concerned, we will do it in an accelerated manner in order to – I repeat – absorb the time, accelerate the constituent time, and not only reform some laws but also form new laws.

We will be careful because here two engines must run in parallel. One feeds the other. I am referring to the second engine, which is the comprehensive and in-depth reform of our Constitution. The revolutionary law of laws to some degree will depend on the comprehensive and in-depth reform of the Constitution. That is why, Madam President, allow me to express my opinion on the urgency of the comprehensive and in-depth reform of the Constitution. I have requested our President Cilia Flores to preside and coordinate the National Commission for the in-depth and comprehensive reform of the Constitution, and she has accepted.

A group of deputies will accompany us, as well as constitutional experts, representatives, spokespersons of the people's power, students, military. It is going to be quite a broad Commission. We are forming it. We already have some documents and I know that there is a lot of work already advanced in this regard.

You know that this Constitution was born in the middle of the storm. You remember that you yourselves even detected, a team of constituent members who, after the debates and the open discussion that took place here, in which all the people and all the social, religious and political sectors participated – there was not a single one who did not participate – after those debates, there in the darkness of an office, a group of members of the Constituent Assembly was modifying articles, betraying the spirit of the Constituent Assembly and of the people. This was detected and discovered.

Even so, many mistakes of the old order, of the old regime remained evident here, as well as other elements that were not well established, well adjusted, or well delineated. That is why I was saying that the Enabling Law, the Revolutionary Law of Laws, and the comprehensive and in-depth reform of the Constitution are like two sister engines of a single machine, of a single plane, or of a single ship. We must work in a very coordinated and accelerated manner because there will be enabling laws that we already have in here as an idea, or there in the notebook, that will only be possible when some reform is made or some part of the Constitution is reformed; because we cannot be above it – it is impossible. For this reason, I tell you, let us summon the constituent power and let us accelerate all this according to the clamor of the people, the popular decision, and the original constituent power of last December 3, 2006.

The people voted, as Cilia rightly said, not for Chávez, no! It is not for Chávez that the people voted, it is for a project, for a path, for a way and Chávez said it a thousand times: we are going the path of socialism. The people voted for the path of socialism. Socialism is what the people want, what the people require; socialism is what the homeland needs.

A few days ago I was rereading Francisco Herrera Luque's novel *En la Casa del pez que escupe el agua*, and, the prologue is written by Héctor Mújica, who concludes: "In this novel, among the characters there is history and there is truth. Cipriano Castro was not overthrown by Gómez, Cipriano Castro was overthrown by oil," and behind oil, I add the gringos. It turns out that in 1908, at the beginning of the year, Castro imposed a fine of 25 million bolívares to that company from Guanoco, the Guanoco asphalt mines. Due to these circumstances and others, there was a break in relations with the United States, and then the illness, and then the trip to Europe and then the compadre Cipriano Castro; and then the gringo ships in La Guaira supported the transition government and then the oil concessions for 50 years; and so they took and plundered our oil, as they plundered our gold and silver and raw materials for so long.

That is why this Revolution proposes, from the beginning, an essential first step: national liberation.

Comrades, friends, compatriots, I may have made many mistakes, and I will try to reduce them in the future, but I say it with an open heart like the savanna where I was born: three thousand days later, Venezuela is free! We are not anyone's colony. Venezuela is liberated.

Article 303 says that the State reserves its sovereignty. For reasons of economic and political sovereignty and national strategy, the State will keep all the shares of Petróleos de Venezuela or of the entity created for the management of the oil industry, but – here comes the "but" – except for the subsidiaries, strategic associations, companies, and any other that may have been created or may be created as a consequence of the business development of Petróleos de Venezuela. This has to be ended. It has to be modified. Nothing is privatized here anymore.

We have to end it here in the Constitution, as well as many, many articles in the economic and political fields, the presidential reelection being one of them. Allow me to bring up the issue here again, and those who have been closer to me or were closer to me in the '90s after Yare, between '90 and '97, surely heard me say this on several occasions: Should Venezuela be divided politically, territorially as it is? Governors, we are going to ask ourselves that question, we are going to shuffle the whole game, all of it. I hope that no governor or deputy will defend regional interests over the national interest.

I repeat the question, is there no other way? Of course there are other ways of territorial organization. I would say that at the state level the situation is not serious, but where it is serious, very serious, is at the municipal level. Does Venezuela need to be divided into as many municipalities as we have today, for example, over there in Táchira? I have always said that in Capacho there are two municipalities in one town, Capacho Arriba and Capacho Abajo. Ah! Old and new. Am I inventing, Mr. Deputy? It is true, and I lived it, I walked all of Capacho. And look, no, this is a Municipal Council, and further down there is another one. Bureaucracy – that is the living Fourth Republic: bureaucracy, corruption, inefficiency.

The model is still intact, so let us change it. That is why I say, let us shuffle, as when one is playing dominoes, let us shuffle the hand. But I invite you all without fear. That is why I say, constituent power is creativity, permanent innovation, otherwise we are going to die little by little, we are going to freeze little by little.

Here it is necessary to bring out philosophy, logic, and knowledge of our reality. Quoting the spirit of Montesquieu's laws, Bolívar said in Angostura: "Should not the laws and the structures be adapted to the nature of things and of the times and of men...?"

There are mayors' offices or municipalities, for example, there in the savanna, that lose sight of each other, have no capacity. There are municipalities that govern an enormous area. There are others that have little territory and are overpopulated, with no capacity to maneuver or make decisions, and almost all the budget goes to bureaucracy. Everyone wants to have advisers, a chauffeur, a good truck, and a palace on top of it all. The Fourth Republic is alive at these levels, but we are going to demolish it, compatriots, we are going to demolish it.

Deep reform is the second constituent engine. We must take the communal power to the constitutional level, and we will not call it the sixth power, no, it must be the first power if we are going to give it an order of priority.

The third great constituent engine is what we have called the great National Campaign of Morals and Enlightenment. Education in all spaces: moral education, economic education, political education, social education, far beyond the school. A moral shake-up in the factories, in the workshops, in the fields, and in the endogenous nuclei. Morals and Enlightenment are the poles of our Republic. I invite all of us to assume this rigorously, not just the government, the Ministries of Education, Higher Education, and Culture. They will be at the forefront, of course, but we must all take up this great National Campaign of Moral and Enlightenment.

The fourth engine has to do with the comments I have been making: We need a new geometry of power, that is, a new way of distributing political, economic, social, and military power over the space of our country. Let us review the political and territorial division of the country, let us innovate, and let us look for formulas that are much more in line with our reality and our aspirations.

And last, there is the explosion of communal power, as I call it, the revolutionary explosion of communal power. All these engines are interconnected with each other. This is the fifth one, and it seems to me the one with the greatest strength: the explosion of communal power. But the generative explosion of communal power will depend on the reform of the Constitution for its development, its impulse, its establishment, its expansion, and its success. It will depend on the enabling laws in a good way, it will depend on the National Campaign of Morals and Enlightenment, it will depend on the new geometry of power, and on other factors.

It is therefore urgent that we assume the task immediately, as we have been doing in the government. The day before yesterday, after the swearing-in, we had a meeting for 6 or 7 hours until after midnight with the ministers, in which I was launching planning guidelines, talking about each of these engines, and giving more details to the ministers to guide their work that begins now.

For example, I will bring forward this reflection about the explosion of communal power. Meditating, observing, reading. "It has occurred to me," to paraphrase Bolívar – "it has occurred to me, as an audacity, taking from ancient institutions, I propose a moral power, it is an innovation…" In the end, the moral power was not accepted. I hope that this innovation of mine will not suffer the same fate as Bolívar's proposal of moral power.

Bolívar's moral power was pushed as an annex to be discussed later, to be consulted with the wise men of the world. They began to stab Bolívar. I don't know how many times Bolívar decreed the freedom of the slaves, and he died in Santa Marta hearing the slaves' hails, and his corpse was taken by four slaves to the old customs house in Santa Marta. That's how Bolívar died, slaves carrying his corpse.

So, this idea has occurred to me, and it will depend on all of us that it does not suffer this fate. I think it is a good idea, forgive me for being immodest, but it will require this: inventiveness, understanding, and conscience. It has occurred to me to accelerate time, as Negri says. Time, Negri says, is not easy to compose. What this means is that the constituent power, activated as a great motor, an unleashed power, passes over space and swallows it up, and converts it into new time, and that time that swallows up space is transfigured into a fundamental actor, into a multitude, into Revolution.

It has occurred to me, Governors, to create a system of federal cities and federal territories. The Constitution says that a federal territory may be created, with conditions. I think we have to review those conditions, and not think of the old federal territories, like Delta Amacuro or Amazonas, a gigantic territory; no, no, no, no. It is not about going backward and turning states into federal territories on a whim; no, no, no, no. The idea has a logic. It is about marching toward a socialist model, and it has occurred to me that there is a path in the territorial aspect, in that effort to build a city in a state, in a region, with the procedure established by the Constitution. Well, let us create a federal territory and, in that federal territory, we would concentrate all the political, economic, and social efforts to move toward a communal city, a city where there is no need for parish councils, where there is no need for mayors' offices or municipal councils, but rather there is communal power.

It would have to be planted in the Constitution and a law and a regulation would have to be made because it is the path to the new.

Flying in a helicopter inspires me. I fly in a helicopter with binoculars looking down and thinking, and it was in a helicopter, looking at a region, that this occurred to me: My God, how this region could rise up! But the mayor, or if the governor, however brilliant he may be, has no capacity. Nor the general of the garrison; one asks so much of the generals, the commanders, the mayors, the governors, and I know that the great majority of them are honest. They work, but they are unable. It is a question of power or lack of power, and it turns out that we have large uninhabited spaces where there is no state, where there is no law, and therefore there is no republic. That is why I was saying we need a new geometry of power in the whole content of the territory.

I believe that we have to continue talking about this and discussing it on another occasion. I am only making this initial reflection, with the hope that the same thing that befell Bolívar's project of moral power will not happen again.

I ask for your support for this idea because I believe in it. I have meditated for hours, upon hours, upon hours. I have made drawings and graphs. I have read old notes, books, theories, theses – but the wisdom is of the collective; it is not mine at all. A system of federal cities marching toward communal cities, and beyond, socialist cities, and that is not decreed – that has to be built.

Minister "Farruco" [Francisco de Asís Sesto Novas] has a very interesting thesis on socialism of the cities, or the socialist cities. Those dreamer socialist architects, and there are many ideas about this – they can be cities that already exist, or they can be territories where there are no cities and we build them totally new, as for example in the Orinoco Belt. I already told the Minister of Petroleum that along the Orinoco Belt and in the middle of it, we are going to build a road and some new cities. Those cities must be born as communal cities and set in a special territory, specially conceived. I call it federal territory and I call it federal city, later communal city; that is the vehicle to, later on, become a socialist city.

This is part of the explosion of communal power. It is not only about the communal councils, but we must also review this in order to strengthen communal cities and communal councils. For example, the communal councils must transcend the local; they were born in the local but they must transcend the local. We should not put limits on the communal councils. The communal councils are instruments or tools of the constituent popular power.

We must drive it and strengthen it.

The communal councils could do well, and the Law of Communal Councils must be modified even though it is only one year old. It has fulfilled a wonderful function; it has started the process.

Now, the communal councils, you compatriots in the neighborhoods and the parishes must transcend, as I said, to a kind of federation of communal councils, so that in a neighborhood there may be twenty communal areas, 20 communities; all this must be regulated in the law and in each community or communal area there is a communal council. But then they must confederate or federate to cover a much larger space, so that they can make deep diagnoses of their communal area, parish, and territory, and so that they can make a plan and a participatory budget based on that diagnosis, and so that they can develop larger works to raise their quality of life in the economic, social and political areas. At the national level, I imagine a confederation of communal councils.

I have had the pleasure of greeting a group of spokespersons of the communal councils who are present here. My greetings to them and the greatest commitment of my heart, of my political will, of my political and revolutionary conscience. You are the soul of the Revolution and of the constituent power.

I beg you, take note of what I want to tell you: Progressively, we, the constituted power (which is what we are), must gradually transfer political, social, economic, and administrative power to the communal power so that we march toward the social state, the communal state, and leave behind the old structures of the bourgeois capitalist state that stops revolutionary impulses and ends up burying them.

That is why I ask that no one oppose this from the outset, and if anyone has doubts, well, as Bertold Brecht said: "Doubt is part of human nature," doubt is necessary. Now, "from it must come winged hope...," said Brecht. Let's fly, it is the time to transform, to relaunch. Communal councils, federations of communal councils.

I told Minister Rodrigo Cabezas, who has also been Chairman of the Finance Committee of the National Assembly, that we still have the LAE [Law of Special Allocations] and the Fides [Intergovernmental Fund for Decentralization], which are laws of the Fourth Republic. We have to modify them. What are the criteria and patterns on which this law is based? We are condemning, among other things, the poorest states to continue being poorer. It is a law of inequalities, this law is the queen of inequalities.

I ask for urgency. I ask for special powers to modify it, because we are going to modify it.

I have at the closing of the year 2006, several billions of bolívares that I am obliged to transfer automatically to the regions. Rejoice, governors, but I ask you, where are the projects? Rejoice, mayors, but I ask you, where are the projects, what is that money going to be used for? Ah! the LAE, ah! the Fides. In some cases, I know that it is used very well and that there are projects, in others, new cars start to appear, in others, special bonuses start to appear, gigantic salaries. I have heard that there are state officials who earn 15 million bolívares a month. What do they do with so much money? Gentlemen of the Assembly, I ask for authorization to regulate and put a ceiling on the salaries and wages of state officials. This is an obscenity.

An obscenity. I am not going to take the president's salary as a reference. I cannot. I should not, because I have practically no expenses. I should not have a salary at all. But some salaries of state officials really seem exaggerated to me, and we have to put a ceiling on them. That is moral, that is ethical. How much does a worker who works much more than us earn? From early in the morning until late at night, he earns the minimum wage: 500,000 bolívares. How can we earn 10 million, or 15 million? For the love of God! In the new state and in the new Constitution, I ask that there not be any autonomous power to make those decisions, none! It cannot be. There has to be a major body making these decisions.

How good it would be if those who earn more than a figure that I dare not comment on, because it would be unfair, but if each one of them, as of today, would send me a letter and tell me: President, I renounce my salary, they gave me so many millions and I will keep so much. I hope, I hope, for examples and manifestations of goodwill.

In sum, for these five engines, I ask for the greatest will of all of us to give them structure. Give them strength and draw strength from the constituent power to accelerate the time and transcend the spaces toward this new era that begins today, the 147th anniversary of the assassination of my General Zamora in San Carlos de Cojedes.

The year 2005 was the bicentennial of Bolívar's Oath in Monte Sacro. The year 2006 that just ended was the bicentennial year of the arrival of Miranda – "The Precursor" – to La Vela de Coro with this yellow, blue, and red tricolor flag, with this dream, with this cry, with this hope.

This period begins today, comrades, compatriots, and for which I will give my all. We are going to conduct elections from below, from the base. I, Hugo Chávez, will register in the constituency that corresponds to me, which is that of my battalion, the "Manuel Palacios Fajardo" high school. If I aspire to be in the National Directorate of a party or region, I must begin by registering in the constituency of my battalion. So that in the Assembly, face to face in the smallest community, delegates are appointed, then delegates to more advanced levels, and assemblies, assemblies, assemblies, and assemblies. This is also the constituent power at the level of the political organization, and believe me that the leaders are the leaders, nobody will disown their leadership. On the contrary, they will be legitimized by the bases and new leaders will emerge, and everything will be positive for the great socialist party that the Bolivarian Revolution requires for this new stage.

I will give myself fully to this new constitutional period of government. We are going to radicalize this process of ours. We are going to deepen this Revolution. We all will adjust ourselves ethically, morally, ideologically, politically, and with efficiency. Alfredo Maneiro used to say "political efficiency and revolutionary quality." Political efficiency and revolutionary quality, in our spirituality, in our dedication to the deepest values. I will try to be, if not at the front, at least in the front line with you, giving the example and making the maximum effort to be the driver of this unbridled people, of this loose, free, and great horse that is the Venezuelan people; a flying horse that decided to be free. It is free and it will be more and more every day.

I was telling you that we are in the bicentennial era. In just three years we will be celebrating the bicentennial of the Revolution of April 19, 1810. We have just three years left. Let us speed up the march to reach the best conditions for the construction of the socialism of the twenty-first century in Venezuela, the best moral conditions, with the best political, social, and economic conditions. To April 19, 2010 and beyond, one year later, to July 5, 2011, the epicenter of the bicentennial era. 200 years later Bolívar's dream will come true in the Orinoco, the dream of Angostura, the delirium of Chimborazo. For this, let us all go forward in unity.

I send greetings to all the presidents, prime ministers, kings, and magistrates of the world, of the countries represented here with dignity by your ambassadors, to His Holiness the Pope, all our greetings, and all our respect. Venezuela wants to continue and will continue to fight for a world of equality, freedom, and justice where there is no more imperialism, a world where the sovereignty of nations and the freedom of peoples are respected. A world of peace. And for there to be peace there must be justice. Respectful greetings to all the governments of Latin America, the Caribbean, and beyond, of the world.

I began with Bolívar, our father who is in the air, in the earth, and in the water, everything bears your name, father, in our abode. Bolívar, our Bolívar, our great Bolívar, our humble Bolívar. One of his last letters impacted me so much that I will carry it with me like a pain as long as I live. In that letter, Bolívar tells Urdaneta and other friends who, writing to him from Cartagena, leaving for Santa Marta; they say to him:

– Go back to Bogotá.

– No, I'm going, I'm going.

And one of the phrases: "What can a poor man do against the world? They ask me to sacrifice what? For the fatherland," he says, "the fatherland does not exist, my enemies took it from me, I have no fatherland to make the sacrifice to." That is how Bolívar died.

One day, after listening to me and these reflections, Fidel, very thoughtfully, said to me: "Chávez that is very hard, I never imagined that Bolívar had come to feel that way," and he said to me that which is like a pledge: "Chávez, neither you nor I can die like that, as Bolívar died, saying, I have no homeland..."

That is why I repeat Bolívar when he said the following, very appropriate to end these words of my heart, this oath of my soul: "The impulse of this Revolution is already given, nothing will be able to stop it. Our party is committed, to regress would be ruin for all. We must triumph by the path of the Revolution and not by any other." Bolívar wrote this to Santander, who later betrayed him on May 30, 1820.

We must triumph by the path of the Revolution, and no other path. He knew that only by that path would they achieve victory. Any other path would lead them to defeat, which sadly, is what happened. 200 years later we have to sing and shout it, as

Alí Primera the infinite singer used to say: With Bolívar, we will triumph by the path of the Revolution.

To victory always. Fatherland. Socialism or death! We will win! Thank you very much brothers, thank you very much sisters.

The communes and the construction of socialism

Speech at Aló Presidente at the Teresa Carreño Theater on June 11, 2009 – Caracas, Venezuela

AS THIS PROGRAM IS *Aló Presidente Teórico*, I brought a sample of books: *Inside a People's Commune*, the Chinese experience, and this wonderful book by Orlando Borrego: *Towards Socialism: Problems of the Economic System and Business Management*. We could read even just half of this other one tonight: *Beyond Capital* by István Mészáros.

We are inaugurating the *Aló Presidente Teórico*; this is the first one.

Today we are with Erika Farías, Minister of People's Power for the Communes, and with the communal councils, the technical working groups for water, urban land committees, and the communal banks. These are all the people's power organizations that have been emerging.

The backbone of what is being born is the communal councils. I invite you all to read, study, strengthen the principles and the roots of our ideological approach and study and deepen the theory, and the ideas. It is impossible for there to be a revolution if there is no revolutionary theory. It is impossible, just as it would have been impossible for this building to exist if it had not been previously guided by a scientific theory.

Nor is this a far-fetched theory. It is about science, technique, technology, methods. That is what the *Aló Presidente Teórico* program is about. In this first program, we are going to talk about people's power, the communal councils and the commune.

That is part of the importance of *Aló Presidente Teórico*. We have to mesh the theory with the experience at the base.

It is necessary to gradually articulate, encompass, clarify, and unify criteria, even within the diversity and the great creative flexibility that is every revolution.

But we have to build the commune as a revolutionary entity, as a territorial, social, political, moral base. If we cannot enunciate it, how are we going to build it?

Those socialist communities, as I understand it, must be the communes. The commune must be the space from which we are going to give birth to socialism. Socialism has to emerge from the grassroots. It can't be decreed; you have to create it. It is a creation of the people, of the masses, of the nation. It is a "heroic creation," said Mariátegui. It is a historical birth, not from the presidency of the Republic.

The commune is the space from where we are going to generate and give birth to socialism from the small. Grain by grain, stone by stone the mountain grows.

The issue of communes has to be transversal; it calls for all fields. It is not just a responsibility of Erika and Chávez, nor of the communal councils.

In 23 de Enero,[1] we are doing a very nice and very good job, with the community, of rehabilitating the public spaces. With that same impulse, we must give life to the communes of 23 de Enero. This is not for later. Do you know what we have to fight here? We have to fight against the so-called Cartesian view of the world, which comes from that man called René Descartes, who established the Cartesian method: dividing reality into parts in order to understand it. But reality is one.

That so-called specialization, that division of labor leads to

---

[1] 23 de Enero is a parish in the city of Caracas

nothing. On a baseball team, for example, I can be the pitcher. That's my job on the team. But how do you understand a pitcher without a catcher? How can you understand it without the first base?

Returning to the issue of the commune, it is everyone's responsibility. Here I want to insist on a theoretical line: It is necessary that we arm ourselves with a holistic vision. Holism is the integral vision. You have to look at the complete reality, and assume it as a whole.

Wherever we are working, we must promote the creation of communes. Each communal council, and the work they are doing, not only physical work, infrastructure work, but social work. We must promote the communes.

Look at this book that a man gave me in one of the many electoral campaigns, a year ago, two years ago, around the Valles del Tuy, it is a somewhat old book from the Chinese Revolution: *Inside a People's Commune* by Chu Li and Tien Chieh Yun, Foreign Language Press in Beijing, 1974.

I had this book photocopied. I'm sure Comrade Chu Li isn't going to be upset. Quite the opposite.

This is only a reference. It is not that we will copy, neither from this nor from other historical experiences of communal systems and communes.

You know that the communal councils were the first step. No, it was just another step in the birth of the entities of people's power. Because that is what the Revolution is: we are advancing, adding knowledge, and experiences. Some are successful, others are not. I remember that some of the first organizations that emerged were the technical working groups on water when Jacqueline [Faría] was in Hidrocapital ten years ago. Then came the urban land committees. They appeared in that sequence, and then came the health committees, and from there the communal councils and the communal banks.

On one occasion, even I myself mistakenly said that all the entities that already existed should join the communal council. It

The communes and the construction of socialism 77

was a wrong view, but I said it myself once. Then I said no, this cannot be forced. It is a creation. In some places yes, in others no. That depends on the people themselves.

It is the people who decide. It is the community that decides. It is not us, it is not Chávez who is going to decide. Chávez can have an opinion, like anyone else, but it is you who decide. This is people's power. This is direct democracy, through people's assemblies, through participation and popular leadership.

When we talk about the precursors of the communes, we have our indigenous peoples, especially in the Venezuelan Andes and the Colombian Andes. But you know that thousands of years ago that was not Venezuela nor was it Colombia. It was a single homeland, the Indian homeland. It wasn't Indian either, because the term "*Indian*" came about because Columbus believed that he came to India, and that is why they called us "Indians." They erased our historical memory.

The other day Evo Morales told me: "Chávez, our original name was *Abya Yala, Pachamama*, our proper name. Until the conquerors arrived and erased us from the historical memory, and imposed their names: the *Indians*." Columbus thought that this was India; but India is on the other side of the world. It's like you come to the town of Sabaneta, and say, "No, I'm in Tokyo."

Thousands of years ago our indigenous peoples lived in communes, they were the communards of the Andes, deeply rooted in the land. The Caribs, of the water and the wind, lived differently. The Andeans lived rooted, as they normally do, to the land, to agriculture, to the mountains.

Also in Paraguay, the communards of Paraguay existed before the arrival of the conquerors. So the commune is not strange to our reality; it is how a good part of our Aboriginal peoples lived. In Central America, the Mayans lived in communes. In South America, the Incas came to form an empire that skimmed the Venezuelan Andes, and spread to the southern cone: the Inca Empire. Some studies even point out that the Inca Empire had socialist characteristics. I have a book that has been with me for many years: *The Socialist Empire of the Incas*, by a French author whose name I cannot remember at this moment.[2]

There is also the example of China, of the communes that comrade Mao Zedong promoted in the Chinese Revolution.

I'm going to read this little page of *Inside a People's Commune*:

What is the people's commune? The people's commune is a creation of the masses. Synthesizing its experiences and creations, Chairman Mao stated, "The people's commune is good." Under the leadership of the Central Committee of the Party, through popular practice and gradual improvement over several years, the people's commune has become a unified national system.

This must be emphasized. Please find today's column of "The grain of corn." Did you read it? That column is not to be missed. I am going to repeat this. We are going to jump from Mao Zedong to Antonio Aponte. I wasn't born yet in 1950, and Mao was already creating communes in the fields of China.

None of us here was born, and Mao Zedong was already making communes, promoting them with the people under this principle, "The people's commune is a creation of the masses." Don't you think this Mao slogan should be repeated everywhere?

It is a creation of you, of the people, of the popular masses. It is not Chávez's, nor is it decreed by the government, nor by Minister Erika Farías, nor by the mayor, nor by the governor, nor by the party. It is by the masses. It is the creation of the masses.

It says here: "The people's commune has become a unified national system." This book was written in 1976. The communes were already 20 years old, or more. I imagine the Venezuelan

---

[2] Louis Baudin, *El Imperio Socialista De Los Incas*, Madrid: La Tarde Libros, 1940.

The communes and the construction of socialism

socialist communes, in the year 2030. That's where we'll go. Then you continue for 20 years. Because our communes have not been born, we are talking about communities and socialism, but we are shuffling, searching, creating, and inventing.

We cannot say that there is a commune in Venezuela today. No, the commune is not just anything. You have to build it, think about it, do it.

20 years from now, our communes must have become a *unified national system*.

What Antonio Aponte says is very appropriate: "The paradox." I recommend reading this column every day, in the newspaper *Diario Vea*. It is good that we reproduce it.

I will read this column from yesterday: "Raising the Local." It has to do with *the national unified system*. A commune is a cell.

A commune must be a cell. But who has ever seen a single cell? One cell has to be next to another, and another, and another to form the body, tissues, and the human body. So it has to be an integrated system of communes, not isolated communes. And that is valid from now on for the communal councils, which are nuclei. You know that the cell has a nucleus. The communal councils are the nucleus of the communes, or one of the nuclei of the communes.

The commune is like a cell. The cells have to branch out and link. They have to form a system, articulate, and give shape to a body. It is the new body of the nation, from below, from the core, which is you.

So what is Antonio Aponte referring to when he writes "Raise the local?" I'll start reading it:

The local, confined only to the local, is counterrevolutionary.

Listen well, and be careful, because one can be a counterrevolutionary, believing that he is the greatest one. One can be acting against the revolution without knowing it. There are many unconscious people who kill not directly but indirectly, by poisoning the waters, for example, by damaging nature.

The local, confined only to the local, is counterrevolutionary. The local, united with the universal in a social and political fabric, is a formidable revolutionary force.

Let's see how:

Socialism restores the social condition of humanity and society. Making humans truly social beings and, therefore, making their organizations social organizations.

In essence, capitalism is the fragmentation of society, making people shipwrecked, isolated, lonely. Of course, the organizations of capitalism will be fragmentative, isolating, raising barriers to communication.

To function, to justify itself, capitalism needs the selfish environment, the war of all against all: competition. That is its reason for being, its vision of the world.

Under penalty of death, of being captured, the Revolution must radically modify the vision of the world proper to capitalism. It must undertake actions that rebuild the social fabric, and for this it is most important to raise the local to the universal level. Establish political, social, economic, organizational, and spiritual relationships from the base to the national level. I would say from the nucleus, from the cell, to the entire national level.

Capillary organizations must know the root causes of their ills and radical solutions, convince themselves that their enemy is the capitalist system, and that the solution is socialism.

You have to be convinced, not just repeat it as a slogan, like some parrots. I'll keep reading:

This being the case, they must be very efficient units in solving local problems – *here he is referring to you, those who are in the micro* – but also efficient in the struggle for the construction of socialism and its defense. Able to mobilize for political goals that go beyond the squalid contours of their existential village, capable of seeing and feeling the world, and of acting to modify it.

You have to connect with the world. We have to help them connect with the world. None of you in a communal council, no matter how far away, no matter how small, no matter how small the community, can be disconnected from what is happening in the world today.

The "Grain of Corn" today is called "The Paradox." It has to do with the same issue. I'm going to read the first sentences:

> The study of the relationship of the local with the universal may seem like an academic distraction, an exercise for theorists without a profession, but it is not like that. In this relationship goes the life of the Revolution and, therefore, its study is of vital importance.

I think the same: here goes the life of the Revolution.

I had thought that we would declare 2010 as the year of the communes. But we could start now, this year, in the second semester with the first rehearsals. I don't want to be rushed, but we could set ourselves next July to start, maybe, in Lara, in Apure, in Falcón, etc.

I propose that we talk about a commune under construction, which is being built. And then, when we have the minimum elements – we do not consider that it will take ten or five years, it will be much fewer – for a commune to be such, [it is then] that the commune starts, the creation of communes.

The communal councils, it must be said, have been like the communal banks, instruments that now allow us to build up the commune. They are like the raw material, like corn for the *arepa*, for example.

Notice the term "commonwealth." Where did the term "commonwealth" come from? Do we consider the commonwealth to be a step toward the commune?

I have never liked the word commonwealth. It is perhaps a matter of personal taste, but it seems to me that it has a certain imperialist connotation. It seems to me that it is a word from the past, and when I say of the past, I mean the worst of the past. The word "union" is from Bolívar. "Union, or anarchy will devour us," said Bolívar. If we do not call ourselves to order and union, we will bequeath a new colony to posterity. Why not, instead of the commonwealth – a concept of the Fourth Republic, that represents values and codes that still live in us and that we sometimes give life without realizing it – why not the union?

I like, for example, the union of communal councils. Because when they tell me "communal councils," I wonder where, for example, urban land committees are located, and what role do they play in these "community councils"?

Each of these communal councils has a territorial scope, and if there are ten, they are grouped together and the territorial scope is enlarged accordingly.

You have to break the old paradigms. Let's not get caught up in the political-territorial division. For example, the municipality of Rómulo Gallegos is in Apure, whose capital is Elorza. If I remember correctly and the limits have not changed, the northern limit is the Arauca. When you cross the river, you are already in another municipality. In the formation of the communes, we must untangle ourselves from that so-called political-territorial division that has nothing to do with the reality of the territory or the reality of radical geography, of socialist geography.

The communes and the construction of socialism

Dead geography is what divides us. The new geography has to unite us. The new geographic vision has to unite us.

When talking about a river, the river does not really divide. The river unites the territories, not only from one shore to the other, but along it is a great path. In that sense, we waste the potential of rivers, which are like the belts on which one is transported at airports. You ride on a boat, you use it as a means of communication between populations. Of course, if you want to go up the river, you put an engine on it and it goes faster.

Let's break the political-territorial division. It does not have to be necessary, then, for a commune to be within the same parish or the same municipality.

There is an example of a commune like this: a commune with a section of Lara and another section of Portuguesa, due to the limits. It doesn't have to be like this in all cases, but I only say that so that we don't get so caught up in it.

I propose that you discuss, and where we already have the "commonwealths," that we go to a higher level and leave behind the "commonwealth of communal councils."

It seems to me that it is a good plan to move toward the communes. And to say toward the communes is to say toward socialism, from below, as it should be, from the small to the large. The connection of the local with the regional, with the national, with the universal.

I have here some figures to review everything we have been doing with regard to the communes. I believe that July – Bolívar's birth month, the month of independence – will be a good month. I would like us to start in July with the first commune trials.

I'm going to ask Erika Farías for a report with her opinion about those communes under construction and the potential communal territories where we could start. They already told me that Lara's are ready, Apure's are ready, Falcón's councils are ready.

Today we are going to deliver some resources.

You know that communal banks are an essential part of this project because they are about creating these opportunities to transfer power to the people, to the communities.

The governors and the mayors will be motivated and will assume the responsibility of transferring more power to the commune. For example, I already talked about the issue of waste collection, which is a job that in the hands of the communes is likely to work very well. Not in the hands of private, contracted companies, which many times do not do their work.

The issue of citizen security, street safety – this is an issue that without the participation of the people, as Minister Tarek El Aissami said in the installation of the National Council for Citizen Security a few hours ago, cannot be fixed. It is something that has no solution without organized participation.

It is about the power of the people to combat these evils in their space. Drug trafficking must be fought there in the community, in the locality, so that neighbors can communicate with spokesmen, with a command post to report criminals and suspicious people in the neighborhood.

Today, within that dynamic of strengthening people's power toward the communes, we will deliver resources to the communal councils for their projects.

In 2008 – these figures must be remembered – 11,728 projects were financed by the state. This is hardly happening in any other country in the world, and less today with the global crisis that exists. General Motors, and I don't know how many companies in the United States, in Europe, collapsed. Unemployment in Europe is horrendous. There are legions of hungry people looking for something to eat in the United States. Capitalism is broken.

Luckily, we are ahead. I think the twenty-first century started early in Venezuela. The twenty-first century began to dawn with the Caracazo. We have been advancing and we have gained space and time. This is not to claim victory, but to take care of what we have achieved.

In 2008, our government financed, only through the communal councils, a total of 4.898 billion bolívares. If we convert this to dollars it is approximately 2.4 billion dollars just through the communal councils.

Today we are going to deliver an amount of 371 million bolívares to a total of 4,017 projects.

In spite of everything, I would not want this year's figure to be lower than last year. So, let's do the math so that we get to at least 5 billion bolívares this year.

If you already have a budget of 4.500 billion, start preparing an application for the second semester. I call on all of us to put ourselves into this savings policy. No to waste. No to consumerism. Let's spend only what is necessary.

The day has to come when the commune manages the commune's water system and electrical system through its organs of people's power. It is their property, it is communal property, and the commune is responsible for it.

Look at, what I said at the beginning: It is not that we will baptize something that is not a commune as a commune, no. Let's not rush. This is so important that we should not rush. We must knead until the dough is ready to be rolled. If it's not ready to be rolled, there's no bread roll.

Let us march without despair. We can make some trials, but believe me, it's not easy at all. It is not enough that we have the communal councils, or that we already have some plots here and now we are the commune.

Who can think of saying that Venezuela today is a socialist country? No, that would be fooling ourselves. We are in a country that still lives in capitalism, only that we have started a path. We are taking steps against the world current toward the socialist project, but that is in the medium to long term. That is why the oligarchy here is determined to stop us; they know we are going there. But they are not going to stop us.

I call on the country, the entire Socialist Party, the allied parties, the social movements, and everyone who feels for the country, to join us in body, soul, nerve, and spirit, and that we defend this Revolution with our lives, if we must. With life itself!

The opposition is desperate. They have launched a new version of what was the Democratic Coordination, so sadly remembered. The unfortunate and falsely named "Democratic Coordination," who was the coup coordinator, the terrorist. They have sent us threats. Because the State is fulfilling its functions, impunity has to end here. Here there are no sacred cows, which cannot be touched. Whoever breaks the law has to be punished according to the Constitution and according to the laws.

Now here are some retired soldiers, some civilians, almost retired, trying to forge another operation. They are looking for soldiers in the barracks, throwing pamphlets in the barracks, spreading rumors that such and such a battalion has risen. About five days ago, there were rumors everywhere, saying "I don't know who rose up in Fort Tiuna," or "in Maracay the paratroopers don't know what else." This is what they want, to generate a buzz and then fish in a troubled river.

They are looking for a way. Whether it is the street blockades, the violence, or "if Chávez is careless, we will break him," said one of them. Well, I am in the hands of God, I am not going to be hidden. I am in the hands of God and the people. Now, as Mario Silva said last night, if this crazed oligarchy were to do any of that, you know what you have to do.

I call on the communities to follow this example, and that we all unite, and beware of sectarianism. If there are inhabitants there who do not participate in politics, who do not belong to any party, well, it does not matter, welcome them.

If someone from the opposition lives there, call him too and let him come to work and be useful. The homeland belongs to everyone, and we must open spaces for it. You will see that with praxis many people are transforming, because it is praxis that transforms. The theory is the theory, but if that theory does not take hold in the soul, in the bones, in the nerves, in the spirit of the human being, then, in reality, nothing will be transformed. We are not going to transform ourselves purely with books.

Books are fundamental, theory is fundamental. But you have to put it into practice. Praxis is what transforms the human being in the end.

When I speak of the political sphere, I speak of the development of the highest possible political power of the communal government in the commune, linked to the national. Remember, we cannot stay in the cell. It is the network, the swarm, the national network, national, and even international.

When I speak of economic power, it is for you to have economic power. And the people will never have economic power until they are the owners of the means of production: land, machinery, technology, knowledge, capital, and labor.

I remind you: People's power is fundamental for the construction of socialism. Revolutionary theory is fundamental for the revolution, for the revolutionary impulse, for the revolutionary course, for the socialist course. Let's study, read, and soak up the theory, individually and collectively, in community councils, readers' circles, the Revolutionary Reading Plan. Let us remember how Martí said: "Be educated to be free." Or as Bolívar said: "Through ignorance they have dominated us more than by force."

So, it must be said: With wisdom, with conscience, we will break all the chains with which they have dominated us.

Long live the communal councils! Long live people's power! Homeland, socialism, or death...! We shall overcome!

Join the side of socialism

Speech at the UN General Assembly on September 24, 2009 – New York, USA

I GREET ALL THE citizens of the world who have come here – as they do every year – for this gathering of such great importance for the world. I am very pleased to be back in New York and at the United Nations following an absence of a few years. I am very grateful for all the cooperation and the manner in which our delegation has been received.

Last night we visited Lincoln Center to see a film made by Oliver Stone during the past year, with a title that already provokes reflection, called *South of the Border*. In this film, you can see President Evo Morales chewing coca leaves with Oliver Stone, and as President Morales says, coca is not the same as cocaine. You can see Cristina Kirchner, the President of Argentina, and General Perón's car, and you can hear what she has to say about events in South America, in Latin America. And you can see Lula, the President of Brazil, in the Guajira region of Venezuela visiting productive centers that we are developing with indigenous peoples of the region, who were exploited for centuries. You will see President Fernando Lugo, a bishop and liberation theologian, living today in the residence occupied for many years by Stroessner, and you can see how a bishop became a president. You can also see Rafael Correa, the President of Ecuador, in Havana with President Raúl Castro. You can see Fidel. You can even see Obama in Trinidad, chatting with a group of us, with his hand held out to us and an open smile.

Join the side of socialism

I think it is an interesting film, one of the many made by this great filmmaker from the United States, Oliver Stone. He had already made two films about Fidel, *Looking for Fidel* and *El Comandante*. There is a lot in this film, and many messages that could help us to decipher the enigmas of the times in which we live.

We stayed behind after the film finished, chatting with a group of people from the United States and other parts of the world. This contact was very instructive and demonstrated the importance of what Fidel calls "the battle of ideas." A lady in her fifties came up to me and said, "I am very happy." She was a North American, very white. A typical United States citizen, born in this country, but she spoke some Spanish. She told me, "I am very happy," and I asked her why. "Because, now having seen this movie, I realize what you are. I thought you were a very bad person."

This person was a victim of the hostile media bombardment, the ideological bombardment, of the United States and of the entire world, whose aim is to turn reality inside out and to turn the world upside down, as Eduardo Galeano put it.

The film is called *South of the Border* and I am taking advantage of this opportunity and that title to tell you that, south of the border, there is a revolution. There is a revolution in South America. There is a revolution in Latin America. There is a revolution in the Caribbean. The world must see this, it must truly realize this and accept it, because it is reality, and it is not going to change. What is more, this is a revolution that goes beyond ideology. It is a geographical and geopolitical revolution. It is a historic revolution. It is part of our times. It has very deep roots. It is a total, moral, and spiritual revolution. We believe that it is a necessary revolution. This revolution is great in both spirit and magnitude, and it is going to keep growing as the days, months and years go by. Why is it great? It is great because it has been a long time coming: centuries of history have led up to this moment in time. It is great in terms of the space that it covers. I was explaining why this revolution is great. First, because of time that has gone by, centuries of battles, of struggles, of hopes, of the suffering of millions and millions of human beings in Latin America and the Caribbean. This revolution is great in the area it covers. This revolution is great in the depth of its foundations. This revolution is great in the masses of people that are joining. No one seeks to slow it down and no one will be able to.

Oliver Stone told me last night that pressure is already being exerted to prevent the American people from seeing the film. Where is their freedom of expression? It is just a movie. How can they be afraid of a movie? But there is already pressure from the monopolies that run the film industry and that operate the theaters. But the movie will be shown elsewhere. Fortunately, we are in the age of computers and telecommunications. We no longer depend on movie theaters run by monopolies.

Anyway, in the film, Evo, speaking with Oliver Stone, recalls a phrase pronounced by a great leader of the Aymara, an ancestor of his who was murdered, just one of the many millions that were murdered by the Spanish, Portuguese, and English invasion, by the European invasion of our continent. I know that all present are aware that when the European ships arrived at the American shores there were approximately 90 million indigenous people living here. Two hundred years later only four million survived. This is one of the greatest genocides in history – the genocide of the continent itself, of Abya Yala, as our indigenous people call it. So, Evo in the movie repeats the sentence uttered by this great Aymara leader, who was drawn and quartered – he was tied to four horses by the arms and legs and he was torn apart, and as he died he uttered a prophecy: "Today I die," said Túpac Katari, "today I die, but one day I will return as millions." Túpac Katari has returned, and we are millions. We are millions.

Nothing and no one can hold back the great South American, Latin American, Caribbean revolution. And I believe the world should support it. The United States should support it. Europe should support it, because this revolution – some brothers and sisters may not have noticed – is the start of the road to salvation for this planet, and to salvation for the human race, threatened as it is by capitalism, imperialism, hunger, and war. This is the necessary revolution. For centuries this has been called "the New World." Now we can truly call it "a new world."

Years ago, I was invited to a conversation with a large group of important leaders. They were important in their own right. They were trade union leaders here in the United States. Some workers were complaining about a biscuit factory that was not paying them. They were striking, and one of them asked me, "Why don't you buy that factory?" And I said, "I'll see. Maybe we can make it a socialist biscuit factory, if Obama gives me permission. Maybe we could do that – buy it, give it to the workers, let them make and distribute the biscuits. Why should there just be one or two capitalists exploiting a lot of people?" That is socialism and that is the path to salvation for this planet.

I'm sure everyone listening to me has read Einstein. Albert Einstein convinced the American President to build the atomic bomb – to begin the research before the Nazis did. Then later he regretted what he had done when he saw the disaster of Hiroshima and the disaster of Nagasaki. But Albert Einstein, after all his years of study, the great scientist, among the greatest scientists ever to have walked the earth, came to the conclusion that the only way for the human race to live on this planet is socialism. Capitalism is the path to extinction for the human species. We as a species have only been around for how long? This is Castro's territory; he knows these figures. But whereas life first appeared here at least three billion years ago, we, the human species, only appeared maybe less than three hundred thousand years ago, hardly 0.01 percent of the time that life has existed on this planet. So, we appear after so long and we're going to wipe out life on this planet?

We've heard it from everybody – Obama, Lula, Cristina Fernández, Al-Gaddafi, Sarkozy – everyone said the same thing. They have all clamored for change. And what is the change?

Capitalism allows no change. Let us not fool ourselves. It is only through socialism that we can bring about genuine change. The revolution in Latin America has it all. It has a strong socialist element. As Mariátegui, the great Peruvian thinker said, it is an Indian American socialism. It is our own socialism. It is the socialism inspired by Simón Bolívar and José Martí. It is a new socialism. It has not been copied from anybody else. There are no manuals for socialism, said Mariátegui. It is a heroic creation that has to be constantly reinvented.

Yesterday we were remembering what a North American president, that is to say, a United States president, said shortly before he was assassinated, on the record, in a speech before the United States Congress. John Kennedy spoke of a revolution in the South, saying that the principal cause was hunger, only a few days later he was assassinated. John Kennedy was not a revolutionary, but he was an intelligent man, just as I think President Obama is an intelligent man. I hope God protects Obama from the bullets that killed Kennedy. I hope Obama will be able to look and see – genuinely see – what has to be seen. It does not smell of sulfur here anymore. That smell has gone. It smells of something else – it smells of hope, and you have to have hope in your heart and believe in the hope.

We cannot destroy this planet. What about our children? What about future generations? Come, let us take on the challenge. Lula was saying yesterday that there was no political will. Those words were whips. I know Lula's will. I am deeply aware of his humane attitude. He is a true brother of mine, and he was right to say what he said, but I would not exactly say that there is no political will. I would say rather that some political will is lacking. Because Lula has it, and we have it, but it has to be increased. It has to continue to grow in the leaders, in society, among the people, among the youth – particularly in the hearts of the young – and the workers, everywhere in the world.

Kennedy said it: There is a revolution in the South. And he

added, "Those who make peaceful revolution impossible will make violent revolution inevitable." Jack Kennedy said that.

Some are trying to block the path to our peaceful revolution. And there's a brave woman, Patricia Rodas, the Foreign Minister of Honduras; please, a hand for this brave Central American woman, from the people of Morazán. Viva Honduras! Viva Morazán! And long live the dignity of the people!

At 1 p.m. exactly, I was jotting down these notes – I don't have much farther to go, Mr. President, don't anybody throw a shoe at me. The Cuban Minister has taken off his shoe to throw it at me. He had some rubber shoes, if you are going to throw a shoe at me throw one of those – I spoke to Manuel Zelaya at 1 p.m. sharp; we started at 1 and finished at 1:13.

While we are here, comrades of the world, there is a president, firm, dignified, who with a small group of people, almost martyrs, was able to escape those trying to carry out a *coup d'état*. The perpetrators of the coup had brought repression to the Plaza Morazán in Tegucigalpa and had taken every single road. They had an entire army. It was as if they had invaded Honduras with their own army – what an indignity. From here I make an appeal – I, who am a revolutionary soldier – to the soldiers of Honduras, to the sons of Morazán, to halt the repression of an innocent people.

While we are here, Manuel Zelaya, the President of Honduras, is in the Brazilian embassy, which has given him refuge. According to what the president has told me, there are more than 200 soldiers surrounding the embassy in the most brutal fashion. Were they trying to go back to the Stone Age? It will not work. Is that what the perpetrators of the *coup d'état* had in mind? They will be swept away by the wind of the new age. The coup cannot succeed, these regressive forces cannot have their way, not in Honduras, not in any of the countries of the Americas. The people have been out in the streets for 90 days, resisting, resisting, resisting.

So, there we have a president, firm in his conviction, with a group of compatriots, with his wife, the First Lady. Apparently, they are not letting food through. The water is cut off every now and then. Luckily there is a cistern with water. In the early hours of this morning, they found Israeli telephone interception equipment on the roof of a neighboring house. Israel has recognized the *coup d'état* government. I think it is the only country in the world that has. They have all kinds of equipment to block signals and jam communications, and they are also trying to create panic among the few people inside the Brazilian embassy, threatening them with incursion into the embassy. Does the Assembly realize how retrograde this is? It is like something from the age of the cavemen. But they will not return.

The people are in the street, protesting. The airport is closed now. Who is behind the *coup d'état*? It is the Honduran bourgeoisie; the state is taken over by the bourgeoisie, by the rich. Four or five wealthy, powerful families own the state. I think we have to pull out our copies of Lenin, his *State and Revolution,* where he talks about the bourgeois State, the control of everything by the bourgeois state including the national congress, the judiciary, and the army.

The people are in the streets, but they are being fired at. Yesterday the president told me that he knows of at least three people in the vicinity of the Brazilian embassy who were killed. And the president is asking for dialogue in order to return to the road to democracy. So let us send the expression of our strongest solidarity to the people of Honduras and President Zelaya.

The United States Government – and this is strange – has not recognized that a military *coup d'état* has occurred. President Zelaya told me today that there is some friction between the State Department and the Pentagon. Yesterday I was reading *Pentagonism*, a book by the great Dominican author Juan Bosch, who was overthrown by imperialism. The Pentagon is the imperial cave. They do not want Obama. They do not want change. They want to dominate the world with their military bases, with all their threats, their bombs, their soldiers, and bases.

Join the side of socialism

The Pentagon is behind the coup in Honduras. President Zelaya was dragged out of his home, out of his bed, at dawn on 28 June, taken to a plane, bundled up by Honduran soldiers under command from the United States base there, in Palmerola. The plane took off from Tegucigalpa and landed at the Palmerola base. They held the Honduran president there for some time. Then they decided to take him to Costa Rica. The American military in Honduras knew about the coup. They supported it. They supported the Honduran military. Hence the contradictions that Obama has to face.

At times we wonder if there are two Obamas – the one who spoke here yesterday and the other the one who supports, or allows his military to support, the coup in Honduras. I want to present this question for thought. Is there one Obama, or are there two? Let us hope the one we heard yesterday will prevail. That is what the world needs. That is what the world is calling for.

What is the backdrop of the coup in Honduras? It has to do with everything we are talking about here – it is the revolution of the South. It is not the kind of revolution where there are columns of guerrillas, heroes like those in the Sierra Maestra, heroes of the high mountains of Bolivia, where Ernesto Che Guevara was.

This is not that kind of revolution. This revolution is different. It does not break out in the mountains with guerrilla groups. No, it starts in the towns among the masses. It is a mass revolution, but it is peaceful and wants to remain peaceful. It is democratic, deeply democratic.

The elite are afraid of the people. They are afraid of true democracy, which Abraham Lincoln, another martyr, defined very clearly in three ideas: Democracy is the government of the people, by the people, and for the people. It is not the government of the bourgeoisie or of the elite, and when the people rise up the thugs are pushed out. That happened in Honduras, and in Venezuela in 2002. It happened in Brazil with João Goulart, and in the Dominican Republic. Why were the peoples of Latin America and of the Caribbean not allowed to build their own future in the twentieth century?

This century is ours. This century, in Latin America and in the Caribbean, we will build our own way, and no one can stop us. No one can stop it. Imperialism must end. At times, one wonders. I once asked Lula what America, our Latin America, would be today if the governments of the United States had not dug their claws into our America to impose a model by violently cutting off the hope and the struggle of millions of people, extinguishing the dawn.

I was born in 1954. Fidel was already in prison, and they were dropping bombs in Guatemala. They invaded the Guatemala of Jacobo Árbenz Guzmán; and then the Bay of Pigs, although they failed there; then this revolutionary Cuba – admirable but blockaded.

I call on Obama to lift the blockade on Cuba. What is he waiting for? Let him do what he says. Or are there two Obamas? Yesterday, Obama said that a political system cannot be imposed on any people and that each people and their sovereignty must be respected. Then what is President Obama waiting for to order the lifting of the brutal and murderous blockade on Cuba? Does anyone have doubts about that? Does anyone think that it is rhetorical? No. There is persecution against businesses in any part of the world that provide even food to Cuba, and now also to Venezuela.

Not long ago, Fidel Castro mentioned in one of his reflections that a company known throughout the world that manufactures and supplies medical equipment did not meet its obligations to the Governments of Cuba or of Venezuela this past year or the one before. They did not send the spare parts for hundreds of pieces of medical equipment that the two governments had bought to bring free quality health care to our peoples. These include 64-row CT scanners and electrocardiogram machines that are now in the poor areas of Caracas. Where the indigenous people live, there are medical facilities. We have 30,000 Cuban doctors there and a free, good health-care system for the people. We tried to quietly find solutions with the company – Philips – but the company has refused to send the spare parts for that high-tech equipment. Why? Under pressure from whom? From the Government of the United States? Is it this Obama or another Obama? Is it Obama one or Obama two? Who are you, Obama? Who are you? I want to believe in yesterday's Obama, whom I saw here, but these things keep happening, and they affect the lives of millions of human beings. Why? In whose name? Why does the United States continue to do that?

It is fear of democracy, just as in Honduras. It is the fear of the Bolivarian Alliance for the Americas that has emerged as a new, novel, solidarity-based integration mechanism. We have formed the Bolivarian Alliance for the Peoples of our Americas, with the governments and countries of Cuba, Nicaragua, Honduras, Venezuela, Ecuador, Bolivia, Antigua and Barbuda, Dominica, and Saint Vincent and the Grenadines. They attack us and try to stop us, but they will not succeed. The Common Market of the South and the Union of South American Nations are being set up and are all part of the great historic Latin American geographic and geopolitical revolution.

Along the same lines are the seven military bases that the United States is going to establish in Colombia. Yesterday, Obama spoke – I have it noted here – about four pillars. Everyone remembers that. So let us accomplish that. I take him at his word. We take the president of the United States at his word: nuclear non-proliferation, agreed? They could begin by destroying all the nuclear weapons that they have. Then go ahead and destroy them.

Obama's second pillar – the first was non-proliferation – is the pursuit of peace. So, President Obama, let us pursue peace in Colombia, in dear sister Colombia. There is a civil war in Colombia. That some do not want to acknowledge it is another matter. There is a long-standing, historical conflict in Colombia.

The United Nations must acknowledge it and consider it, and we all should extend a hand to Colombia, while of course respecting its sovereignty, to pull it and help it out of that tragedy that our brother people are experiencing.

I mentioned that peace to Obama in front of Lula in Trinidad and Tobago at the Summit of the Americas. Let us seek peace in Colombia. If only peace were achieved in Central America, in Guatemala. When I was an active soldier, I was in Guatemala. That was war, with thousands and thousands dead and disappeared. Look at El Salvador and Nicaragua. And now Daniel Ortega is back in government after almost 20 years. The Sandinista people brought him back.

Farabundo Martí and the people of El Salvador brought President Funés to the presidency of that sister republic. Peace was achieved – I know President Arias is here – and if peace was achieved in Central America, my God, why can peace not be achieved in Colombia? This is one of the greatest desires of my life. I am Venezuelan, but I feel like a Colombian – the Colombia of Bolívar, the Colombia of Miranda, our Colombia.

Is President Obama thinking of seeking peace – his second pillar – with seven more military bases in Colombia? These seven bases are a threat, not only for the possible peace in Colombia, but also for peace in South America. We are right – we the Governments of South America – to have said, each in our own way and in our own degree of intensity, how concerned we are about the installation of these seven American military bases on Colombian territory. I would like to denounce it and point it out. I ask President Obama to think about it and to apply his pillars.

Let us promote peace. The United Nations could set up a peace commission in Colombia or Venezuela. Naturally, we would cooperate, I am sure; all countries that want peace. We do not want any more war among ourselves.

There is another topic that Fidel touches upon in his reflections

Join the side of socialism

of September 21. It has to do with climate change. I am going to take another two minutes, Mr. President, to insist on this point. Some people think this is a metaphysical concern, it is for intellectuals. No, we are destroying our planet.

Fidel says, in his piece entitled "A species in danger of extinction", from September 21, 2009, "At the international environmental conference held by the United Nations in Rio de Janeiro" – that was in 1992; I remember because I was in jail at the time – "I stated, as the then head of the Cuban state, 'A species is in danger of extinction – man.'" Fidel goes on to say:

> When I uttered and backed up those words, received and applauded by the heads of state in attendance – including the president of the United States, a Bush less dismal than his son George W. – they still believed that they had several centuries to confront the problem. I myself did not envision a date any closer than 60 or 80 years.
>
> Today we are dealing with a truly imminent danger and its effects are already visible.
>
> Average temperatures have increased 0.8 degrees centigrade since 1980.

That is scientific data, according to the NASA Institute for Space Studies – 0.8 degrees in the last almost 30 years. Fidel continues,

> The last two decades of the twentieth century were the warmest in hundreds of years. The temperatures in Alaska, the Canadian west, and eastern Russia have gone up at a pace that doubles the world average. Arctic ice has been quickly disappearing and the region can experience its first completely ice-free summer as soon as the year 2040. The effects are visible in the 2-kilometer-high masses of ice melting in Greenland,

the South American glaciers, from Ecuador all the way to Cape Horn, fundamental sources of water, and the gigantic ice cap covering the extensive area of Antarctica.

Current carbon dioxide concentrations have reached the equivalent of 380 parts per million, a figure surpassing the natural range of the last 650,000 years.

We are destroying our planet. We must be aware of this, and we must act, as Lula stated at the third meeting yesterday. With respect to climate change, Lula said there is no will. The most developed countries do not want to make decisions. But Obama says they do. But we are told that the United States is going to make some decisions. Please do, Mr. President, do that. Now it is time to move from words to action. Let us save this planet. Let us save the human race.

Let us hope that the summit in Denmark in December will produce decisions, truly compelling ones. Venezuela is willing to accept those decisions. Venezuela calls on everyone to make decisions proportionate to the extent of their responsibility.

What is the basic cause of this contamination? It is hyper-consumption. We are exhausting petroleum, gas, and other fossil fuel reserves. Reserves that accumulated over millions of years are being burned in less than a century.

And that of course has to do with the economy. I shall not read this document, Mr. President. I shall merely refer to it. It is the Stiglitz report. I invite the Assembly to analyze it. Yesterday the President of France also invited the Assembly to analyze it. It is thanks to him that the report of the Stiglitz Commission exists. But it is nothing more than a mere gesture.

The report contains 12 recommendations. Let us assess them. I think that they address the substance, although they do not question the capitalist model. We socialists do question that model, but let us talk about it, let us find solutions in consensus for the present circumstances and later for the medium and long terms.

In its recommendations, the Stiglitz report says, first, that we should look at income and consumption to assess material well-being. Second, it recommends prioritizing the family perspective; third, taking into account inheritances; fourth, giving more importance to redistribution of income beyond the average. Fifth, it recommends expanding indicators of non-commercial activities. For example, certain services such as childcare, bricklaying, plumbing and carpentry appear in national accounts only if they are carried out by a salaried person.

Delegates know that this has to do with accounting for the gross domestic product (GDP). These are merely capitalist mechanisms. According to the report, the following is certain: GDP rises with traffic, while the anxiety of the people also rises, just as the unhappiness of passers-by and passengers in traffic rises as they lose precious time in the traffic.

GDP rises. Why is it rising? It is rising because more gasoline is consumed. Moreover, pollution increases. We know why. The capitalist world has created measuring methods for the economy that are destructive. That is why I think the Stiglitz report offers important considerations. Here, in its second point, it says that we should establish a battery of indicators for the environment and for climate change.

Turning to the economy, this report is very timely. Let us now adopt it, and above all, governments, particularly governments of the most developed countries – I think they are meeting in Pittsburgh today, not as the Pittsburgh Pirates, but as Presidents of the G20 – should discuss it. Tomorrow I will ask Lula and Cristina how the meeting went, because they are coming to Caracas on their way to Margarita Island for the Africa-South American summit.

The economy, the economy, the economy. We are in favor of socialism, but let us discuss it and talk about indicators and methods and modes of production. As President Obama said yesterday with regard to his fourth pillar, we need an economy that serves human beings. Well, President Obama, that is called socialism. Come over to the side of socialism, President Obama, come join the axis of evil and we will build an economy that truly serves human beings. It is impossible to do that with capitalism. Capitalism only benefits a minority and excludes the majority. Besides, it destroys the environment and destroys lives. That is capitalism.

Finally – and I think I have now been speaking for my allotted ten minutes – I will end with a phrase of Lula's. He was the first speaker in the Assembly yesterday. He said there is no political will. I have already commented on that, and I would add to it because I know Lula and I know exactly what he said to us. He is calling upon all of us to strengthen our political will.

Unlike other governments elsewhere, which have hesitations and do not want to change despite the terrible crisis in which we are living, we in southern America have a lot of political will – here I am speaking for Venezuela and, I know, also for South America, for Latin America – a tremendous political will for true change.

I recommend this book by István Mészáros, a great Hungarian philosopher and thinker who has been a professor at various universities in London for many years: *Beyond Capital: Toward a Theory of Transition*. I think the book is among the greatest writings of the twentieth century. It is a complete renewal of socialist theory. In one of the interesting chapters, Mészáros quotes another great person, Karl Marx. We must not be afraid of Karl Marx – he was the Einstein of politics. Yes, he was demonized, but Karl Marx was right about so many things.

Quoting Marx, Mészáros says in this book that crises act as a general threat and thus urgently lead us beyond presuppositions toward a new historic paradigm. We need a new historic paradigm. For years we have been hearing about a new world, but what actually exists is this old, moribund order. We need a new order to be born, a new historic paradigm, a new political paradigm, a new global paradigm. Yesterday Al-Gaddafi said here that we need a new institutional framework, a new economy, a new society, but truly new – a world that is new.

Now, I think Lula said yesterday that we must become the midwives of history. I agree. I would add to what Lula said. Has the birth already started? The birth is not a future event; it is here. Let us be, as Comrade Lula said, midwives of the new history, prevailing over those who would bury it. Let us struggle on the planet for the birth of this new history, this new time, this new multipolar, free world, this economy at the service of all people, not of minorities, this world of peace.

I am a Christian. One day Christ said, "My kingdom is not of this world." It is of a future world, the reign of love among us, where we can truly live as brothers and sisters.

Last Sunday in Havana – and I will put my little books away and I will wind up now – on the Revolution Square there was a great concert, the "Concert for Peace", with Miguel Bosé, Juanes, Olga Tañón and Cuban singers. Silvio Rodríguez was there – the Great Silvio – and they sang to the whole world. Some people in Miami went crazy and tried to destroy Juanes' CDs – that great Colombian – just because he had gone to sing on the Plaza of the Revolution. How far does the madness go? Fortunately, they are a minority. Silvio was there with his guitar, and I am sure he sang, "This era is giving birth to a heart." He ends his song, *Cita Con Angeles*, like this: "Let us be a tiny bit better and a little less selfish."

Only through the path of socialism

Speech at the XV UN Climate Change Conference on December 16, 2009 – Copenhagen, Denmark

MR. PRESIDENT, LADIES AND gentlemen, excellencies, friends, I promise not to talk more than the one who spoke the most this afternoon. I would like to make a comment on the point mentioned by the delegations of Brazil, China, India, and Bolivia. We were asking for the floor, but it was impossible. Bolivia's representative said: the presented text is not democratic, it is not inclusive.

I had just arrived, and we were all just taking our seats when we heard the president of the previous session saying that there was a document available, but nobody knows about it. I have asked for the document. We still do not have it, and I believe that no one knows about this "top secret" document. Certainly, as the Bolivian comrade said, this is not democratic nor inclusive.

Ladies and gentlemen, is this not the reality of the world? Are we living in a democratic world? Is the world's system inclusive? Can we expect something democratic from the current world system? What we are living on this planet is an imperial dictatorship and we will continue to denounce it. Down with the imperial dictatorship! Long live the peoples, democracy, and equality on this planet!

This is an example of exclusion. A group of countries think they are superior to us, we of the Global South, the Third World, the Underdeveloped World. Or, as the great friend Eduardo Galeano says: We are the countries that were run over by the train of history. So don't be surprised. There is no democracy in the world. We are here, once more, observing the powerful evidence of the world imperial dictatorship.

Later on, two young men took the stand, and luckily the security officers behaved decently. A few pushes and they cooperated, didn't they? Do you know a huge crowd is gathered outside? Of course, there is no room inside for so many people. I have read news reports saying that some people have been arrested and that there are some intense demonstrations in the streets of Copenhagen. I want to say hello to all these people out there, most of them young people.

These are young people who are concerned – obviously more concerned than we are – about the world's future. Most of us here are approaching the deadline. They are just beginning the track and are really concerned. We could say, Mr. President, quoting the great Karl Marx, that a specter haunts the streets of Copenhagen. And I think this specter silently haunts this hall. It's over there, among us, passing through the corridors, emerging from below, it rises. This is a frightening specter that no one wants to mention. It's the specter of capitalism, and no one wants to mention it.

It's capitalism, and there, outside, you can hear the people roar. I was reading some slogans painted in the streets by the youth. I heard some of them, and I wrote two of them down. Two powerful slogans, among others. One:

Change the system, not the climate!

I'll take it for us. Let's not change the climate, let's change the system! And as a result, we will save the planet. Capitalism and its destructive development model are destroying life. It wants to destroy humankind.

The other slogan makes us reflect. It's in tune with the banking crisis that has swept the world and still affects us, and how the rich northern countries helped bankers and big banks. In the United States alone, the aid to save the banks is astronomical. They say in the streets,

> If the climate were a bank, it would have already been saved.

I think it's true. If the climate were one of the biggest capitalist banks, the rich governments would have already saved it.

I think Obama hasn't yet arrived. He received the Nobel Peace Prize on the same day he sent 30,000 more soldiers to kill innocents in Afghanistan. Now the US president comes here with the Nobel Peace Prize. The US has the machine to fabricate bills, and dollars and have saved (well, they think they have saved) banks and the capitalist system. This is what I wanted to say while I was sitting over there, and we were raising our hands to join Brazil, India, Bolivia, and China in their interesting position, which Venezuela firmly shares, as well as the member nations of the Bolivarian Alliance. But we were not allowed to speak. Thus, please don't count these minutes, Mr. President.

I had the pleasure of knowing the great French writer Hervé Kempf. I recommend this book: *How the Rich Are Destroying the Earth*. This is why Jesus Christ said, "*It is easier for a camel to go through the eye of a needle, than for a rich man to enter into the kingdom of God.*" The rich are destroying the Earth. Do they think they will go to another planet when they destroy this one? Do they have plans to go to another planet? There is no other planet in the horizon of the galaxy so far. I have just received this book, Ignacio Ramonet gave it to me. Kempf has a remarkable phrase which reads as follows: "*We will not be able to reduce the global material consumption if we do not make the powerful people go downstairs and fight inequality. It is necessary to add the principle the situation requires to the useful ecologist principle when people reflect globally and act locally. Less consumption and better sharing."* This is good advice given by this French writer Hervé Kempf.

Now then Mr. President, climate change is undoubtedly the most devastating environmental problem of this century: floods, droughts, strong storms, hurricanes, thaws, the rise of the average sea level, acidification of oceans, and heatwaves. All these phenomena enhance the impact of the global crises striking us. Current human activity goes beyond the threshold of sustainability and jeopardizes the life of the planet, but we are also deeply unequal in this. I want to recall: The richest 500 million people – 500 million – that's to say 7 percent of the entire world population, is responsible for 50 percent of polluting emissions, while the poorest 50 percent is responsible for only 7 percent of polluting emissions. For this reason, I find it a little strange that the United States and China are put at the same level. The United States has nearly 300 million inhabitants. China has five times the population of the United States. The United States consumes over 20 million oil barrels per day; China only consumes 5.6 million oil barrels per day. We cannot demand from the United States the same that we demand from China. We have to discuss these issues. I hope we, the heads of state and government, can sit down and really discuss these issues.

Likewise, Mr. President, 60 percent of the ecosystems of the planet are damaged and 20 percent of the earth's crust is degraded. We have impassively witnessed deforestation, land conversions, desertification, alteration of drinking water systems, excessive exploitation of sea resources, pollution, and loss of biological diversity.

The excessive exploitation of the earth outnumbers by 30 percent our capacity to regenerate it. The planet is losing its capacity to self-regulate. More waste than we can process is dumped every day. The survival of our species gnaws at the conscience of humanity. Despite the urgency, two years of negotiations to reach a second commitment period under the Kyoto Protocol have elapsed. The second period of commitment under the Kyoto Protocol has concluded, and we are attending this meeting without a real and significant agreement.

By the way, regarding the text that is coming out of the blue, the Chinese and Venezuelan representatives, as well as the Bolivarian Alliance [ALBA] countries, say that we do not accept any text besides those that come from the working groups of the Kyoto Protocol and the Convention. These are the legitimate documents that have been thoroughly discussed these past years.

I don't think any of you have slept, nor have you eaten in these past hours. I do not think it is logical that a document appears out of the blue now.

The scientifically supported objective of reducing pollutant gas emissions and achieving a long-term cooperation agreement clearly seems to have failed for the time being.

And what's the reason? We have no doubt. The reason is the irresponsible attitude and the lack of political will of the most powerful nations on the planet. I do not want anyone to be offended. I want to quote José Gervasio Artigas when he said: "With the truth, I don't offend or fear." But it really is an irresponsible attitude of exclusion. It is an elitist approach to a problem that concerns all of us and can only be solved by all of us.

The political conservatism and selfishness of the large consumers, the richest countries, denote a high insensitivity and lack of solidarity with the poorest, the hungriest, and the most vulnerable to diseases and natural disasters. Mr. President, it is essential that we reach a new and unique agreement applicable to totally unequal partners because of the extent of their contributions, and their economic, financial, and technological capacity. It must be based on the utmost respect for the principles contained in the Convention.

The developed countries should take on binding, clear, and concrete commitments to substantially reduce their emissions, and assume obligations to provide financial and technological assistance to the poorest countries, to fight the destructive dangers of climate change. In this sense, the singularity of the island states and less developed countries should be fully recognized.

Mr. President, climate change is not the only problem affecting humanity nowadays. Other scourges and injustices beset us. The gap between rich and poor countries has not stopped growing in spite of the Millennium Goals, the Monterrey Summit, and all the other summits. As the President of Senegal said here, exposing a great truth, we have only promises and unfulfilled promises, and the world continues its destructive march.

The total income of the 500 richest individuals of the world is higher than the income of the 416 million poorest people. The 2.8 billion people living in poverty with less than 2 USD per day represent 40 percent of the world's population, and they only receive 5 percent of the world's income. Today, around 9.2 million children under five die every day, and 99.9 percent of these deaths take place in the poorest countries. Child mortality amounts to 47 deaths per thousand children born alive, but it only amounts to 5 per thousand in rich countries. Life expectancy in the world is 67 years. In the rich countries, it is 79, while it is 40 in some poor nations. In addition, there are 1.1 billion people with no access to drinking water, 2.6 billion with no cleaning services, over 800 million illiterates, and over 1 billion hungry people. That's the world scenario.

What is the cause? Let's talk about the cause. We should not avoid responsibilities. We should not avoid the depth of this problem. I'll bring it up again. The cause of this disastrous panorama is the metabolic, destructive system of capital and its model: capitalism. I want to briefly read aloud the teachings of that great liberation theologian from Brazil, Leonardo Boff. Leonardo Boff says the following on this issue: "What's the cause? Oh, the cause is the folly of seeking happiness through material wealth and endless progress by using science and technology, with which all the resources of Earth can be exploited with no limits." He also quotes Charles Darwin and "natural selection," the survival of the fittest, but we know that the fittest survive on the ashes of the weakest.

We always have to recall Jean-Jacques Rousseau. He used to say: "Between the strong and the weak, freedom oppresses." That's the reason why the empire talks about freedom: the freedom to oppress, invade, assassinate, annihilate, and exploit. That's its freedom. And Rousseau adds the revealing phrase: "Only the law liberates."

There are some countries that are playing for there to be no document here, precisely because they do not want a law. They do not want a norm, because the non-existence of that norm allows them to exercise their exploitative freedom, their overpowering freedom.

Let's make an effort and put pressure here and in the streets so that a commitment is made, and draft a document that will commit the most powerful countries on the earth.

Well, President, Leonardo Boff asks: "Can a finite earth stand an infinite project?" The capitalist thesis, infinite developmentalism, is a destructive model. We must admit it.

Then, Boff asks another question: "What could we expect from Copenhagen?" Just this simple confession: We cannot continue the way we are. And a simple purpose: Let's change our course, let's do it without cynicism, without lies, without double agendas, without arbitrary documents, with an honest and truthful attitude.

From Venezuela, we ask, Mr. President, ladies, gentlemen, how much longer are we going to tolerate such injustices and inequality? How much longer are we going to tolerate the current international economic order and the current market mechanisms? How much longer are we going to allow epidemics like HIV/AIDS to demolish entire populations? How long are we going to stand by and allow the starving to be unable to feed themselves and their children? How long are we going to allow millions of children to continue to die of curable diseases? How long are we going to allow armed conflicts that massacre millions of innocent human beings in order for the powerful to appropriate the resources of other peoples?

The peoples of the world demand an end to aggressions and wars, against the imperialists, against those who seek to continue to dominate the world and exploit us. No more imperial military bases, nor *coup d'états*. Let's build a fairer and more equitable economic and social order. Let us abolish poverty, let us stop the high levels of emissions immediately. Let us halt environmental deterioration and avoid the great catastrophe of climate change. Let's join in the noble task of becoming freer and more united.

Mister President, almost two centuries ago, a universal Venezuelan, liberator of nations and precursor of consciousness pronounced an apothegm full of will: "If Nature is opposed, we will fight her and make her obey us..." This was Simón Bolívar, the Liberator.

From Bolivarian Venezuela, on a day like today, ten years ago we lived through the hardest climate disaster of our history, the Vargas tragedy. From that Venezuela whose Revolution aims at conquering justice for all its people, we say that there is no possible way out but socialism. Socialism is the other specter mentioned by Marx. It is also among us. For want of a better word, it is a counter-specter. I have no doubt that is the way toward the planet's salvation. Capitalism, on the contrary, is the way toward hell, the world's destruction. And Venezuela faces thus the threats of North American imperialism.

From the countries of ALBA, Bolivarian Alliance for the Peoples of Our America, we urge, respectfully, and on behalf of many in the world, the governments and peoples of the earth, in the words of Bolívar, the Liberator: If the destructive nature of capitalism opposes us, we will fight it and make it obey us. Let us not wait with folded arms for the death of humanity.

History calls us to fight. If capitalism resists, we are obliged to fight against it and to open new ways toward the salvation of humanity. It is up to us, to raise the banners of Christ, of the Prophet Mohammad, of equality, of love, of justice, of humanism, of the truest and deepest humanism. If we do not do so, the most marvelous creation of the universe, the human being, will disappear.

This planet is billions of years old and has existed for billions of years without us. That is, it does not need us to exist. Now, we cannot live without the earth, and we are destroying the *Pachamama*, as Evo says, as our indigenous brothers of South America say.

Finally, Mister President, to conclude, let us hear Fidel Castro when he said: There is a species in danger of extinction: the human being.

Let us hear Rosa Luxemburg when she said: Socialism or barbarism.

Let us hear Christ when he said: Blessed are you who are poor, for yours is the kingdom of God.

Mister President, Ladies, Gentlemen, let us make of this planet not the grave of humanity, but a heaven of life, peace, and fraternity for the whole of humanity.

Strike at the helm

Speech at the Council of Ministers at the Miraflores Palace on October 20, 2012 – Caracas, Venezuela

WE ARE SPEAKING, ABOVE all, on the theme of economics. We are looking over papers, documents, plans, projects. We are closing one cycle and opening up a new cycle after the Bolivarian victory on October 7th, which has broadened the political horizon and brought us a people's victory, guaranteeing our nation's stability.

I was reading somewhere that Venezuelan bonds have shot up. The world knows that PDVSA [Petroleum of Venezuela] now appears to be the second-largest company among Latin America's top 500, making it one of the largest in the world – a solid position – and Venezuela continues to occupy a place that it deserves. This is only possible (and will continue to be possible) along this course, along these horizons, along these paths, along these roads of the construction of socialism.

I have a book here written by István Mészáros. In Chapter 19, called "The Communal System and the Law of Value," there is a sentence that I underlined a while ago that speaks of the economy, of economic development, and of the social impulses of the revolution: "The yardstick," says Mészáros, "of socialist achievements is the extent to which the adopted measures and policies actively contribute to the constitution and deep-rooted consolidation of a substantively democratic…mode of overall social control and self-management."

Therefore, we arrive at the issue of democracy. Socialism in its essence is truly democratic while, on the other hand, there is capitalism: quintessentially anti-democratic and exclusive, with the imposition of capital by the capitalist elite. Socialism is none of these things. Socialism liberates. Socialism is democracy, and democracy is socialism – in politics, the social sphere, and in economics.

Our dear minister, friend and teacher, Jorge Giordani, also says this, in his book *The Venezuelan Transition to Socialism*. Jorge speaks about some of the decisive factors in the transition. One of them is the transformation of the country's economic base in order to make it fully and fundamentally democratic, because the economic base of a capitalist country is not democratic. It is anti-democratic. It is exclusive. That is how it generates great wealth for a minority, for the elite, the bourgeoisie, and for the big monopolies. This also how it generates poverty and squalor for the vast majority of the population.

The problem is an economic one. It is impossible to separate the social from the economic. I always give water as an example, H_2O, hydrogen, and oxygen; the economic and the social.

Here is the book, *The Venezuelan Transition to Socialism*, on the conditions which guide the passage, that is to say, the transition: "When dealing with revolution or a productive transformation," Giordani says, "as far as the productive transformation is bound to an accumulative model, it will be defined by five aspects:

1. The modification of the productive base of the country, seeking a higher level of the democratization of economic power.
2. A change in the role of the State, so that the accumulative process is able to begin to achieve the fulfillment of the basic necessities of the majority of the population and the defense of its sovereignty.
3. The incorporation of mechanisms of self-governed productivity at a collective level.

4. The use of democratic planning as a regulatory mechanism for productive relations.
5. Accentuating the autonomous position of the country while facing the internationalization of the capitalist system.

These are the elements that help to guide the transformation, and they are what we are going to be talking about today: the economy, and how now, at the beginning of this new cycle, we must become more efficient in the construction of a new political, economic, social, and cultural model: the revolution.

This effort that we have undertaken and that we continue to take on is a serious one, and it must be taken even more seriously. That is what Jorge is saying. We must modify the productive base of the country in a way that assures an economic democracy. For example, here in the Miranda Airbase, in La Carlota, a pole of scientific-technological development is taking form, and this is one of the strategic lines of the theme we are discussing. Science and technology, independence – it is all related.

Let us recall the five major historic objectives of the Program for the Homeland [*Programa de la Patria*] that we will now begin to apply.

This concerns the steps that we have taken, which is why we speak of transition, of stages. None of this existed in Venezuela and none of this would exist in Venezuela if capitalism were imposed upon us, if we reverted once again into the colony we once were. This is why the political revolution comes before the economic one. It must always be this way: first the political revolution, political liberation, and then the economic revolution. We must maintain political liberation; and from that point, the political battle is a permanent one, the cultural battle, the social battle.

Socialist democracy of the twenty-first century

We are touching on the key points of this project, which if we do not understand and take on well, we may do good things, but not necessarily what is required to progressively and firmly leave behind the capitalist model of exploitation and create a new model: socialism that is Venezuelan, Bolivarian, and of the twenty-first century.

It is a new cycle of the transition; the construction of socialism, of our model. We should territorialize the models. I imagine, for example, a sector of Sarría, the Calle Real de Sarría, the buildings and the bakery, the PDVAL [Venezuelan Production and Distribution of Food] and the Farmapatria [state-run pharmacy] are new elements, like grafts. Now colleagues, comrades, if this element did not form part of a systematic plan, of something new, that works like a giant spiderweb covering the new territory – if it didn't work this way it would all be doomed to fail. It would be absorbed by the old system, which would swallow it up, because capitalism is an enormous amoeba, it is a monster.

That is why the socialism of the twenty-first century, which has resurfaced here as if from the dead, is something new. It has to be truly new. One of the things that is fundamentally new in our model is its democratic character, a new democratic hegemony that obliges us not to impose, but rather to convince, and that is what we were discussing – the subject of the media, of communications, of our arguments – so that what we are presenting today, for example, can be perceived by the entire nation; how to achieve it, how to make it happen.

Cultural change. All of this must have an impact on a cultural level, which is vital for the revolutionary process and for the construction of a twenty-first century socialist democracy in Venezuela.

Self-criticism for rectification

Now the self-criticism: On many occasions I have insisted on this. I read and read, and all this is very nice and well done, I don't doubt it, but where is the commune? Maybe the commune is only for the Ministry of the Communes? I have often thought that I will have to eliminate the Ministry of the Communes. Why? Because many people think that the Ministry is the one that deals with the communes.

This is a very serious error that we are committing. We will not comment on it any further. We will revise it. I signed a decree creating something that is a superior entity to the communes. Where is this entity? It has not served its function.

Nicolás [Maduro], I entrust you with this task as I would entrust my life to you: the communes, the rule of law, and the justice system. There is already a Law of the Communes, of communal economy. So, how will we make it happen…?

I asked the same question in Ciudad Caribia: Where is the commune, no, not the commune, but the communes? Where will we create the communes, the new ones? And in Ciudad Belén, we continue to create housing, but we do not see communes anywhere. Not even the spirit of the commune, which at this point is much more important than the commune itself: the cultural commune. Do you understand? Will I continue to preach in the wilderness for things like this? All of us here are a part of this, all of us, starting with me President of the Republic. Here in Miraflores there should already be a commune. We are all involved in this; it is part of the soul of this project.

Self-criticism is used to clarify, not to speak empty words, as if we were to throw our criticisms into a void. It is used so we can act now, ladies and gentlemen, ministers. The communes dictate that we search out the Law of the Communes, that we read it, and study it. Many people, I am sure, haven't read it because it is believed that it isn't about us. Many of us haven't read the Law of Communal Economy because we think no, this doesn't have anything to do with me.

You may ask, which are these so-called communes under construction? I am sure that in the majority of these projects that we are developing, be they small, medium, or large, from housing, new cities, centers of scientific and agricultural development, like in the plains of Maracaibo, in the municipality of Mara, even in the state of Sucre, where the large sardine processing plant that we recently opened is located, even in the glass businesses that we expropriated, la Faja de Orinoco [the Orinoco Belt], the communes do not exist. Where will we search for them? On the moon? Or on Jupiter?

Friends, permit me to be as tough as I can be, and as I should be, regarding this new self-criticism on this topic. Rafael Ramírez, for example, should already have around 20 communes in the Faja de Orinoco, but the PDVSA doesn't believe that they should have anything to do with them. The problem is a cultural one, friends. And I mention PDVSA in full recognition of this great industry.

The communes. Once I actually had Carmen Meléndez make, who knows how many copies, of Mao Zedong's writings on communes from his *Little Red Book*. Now I want to make 30 more copies to give, once again, to each minister. It seems as if no one ever read them, since I never even received one page of commentary regarding them.

Self-criticism: Either independence or nothing, either the commune or nothing. Or what exactly is it that we are doing here? This is where we need the Mission of Culture to concentrate its fire, like artillery.

The spirit of the micro-missions is to concentrate that fire. Someone tell me, how many ministers – you my dear friends – have gone to spend three days in a neighborhood. Tell me who has done so. I can't set the example, as much as I would like to, but you could. You could go to Caño Cuibarro and spend three days to see what is happening with the Cuiba Indian's project, or you could scatter yourselves around Sarría. Any minister or vice-minister could live there for a few days or go back and forth from house to house. This does not only have to take place during an electoral campaign, going street corner to street corner. Haven't you seen the amount of paper that I am bombarded with, that falls in my truck everywhere I go? Now they throw the paper with rocks, so that it reaches me, or with an arrow. Once there was an arrow with a piece of paper on the tip: "Chávez help me…"

So, the commune, popular power, does not come from Miraflores nor does it come from the Office of the Ministry. This is not where the problem will be solved.

We do not believe that because we are going to open the Cemento Cerro Azul factory, or the industrial manufacturing equipment factory in Guanare, or the computer factory, or the satellite factory, or this factory or the other that we have just finished, no. Nor because we have nationalized the cement industry….

Be careful. If we are unable to realize this, we are done for, and not only are we done for, but we will be the ruin of this project. Those of us here, those present, face a historical responsibility. Each time you go to the bathroom, or wherever there is a mirror, look at yourselves in the face, look yourselves in your eyes. I will be the first to do it.

Socialism cannot be decreed

Factories constructed with capitalist ends carry the indelible mark of their "operating system," the division of the social hierarchies of work from which they were built. A productive system that aims to activate the full participation of the associated producers, the workers, requires a multiplicity of parallel producers, who are coordinated in a suitable way, as if in a corresponding operating system that is radically different from the centrally operated alternative of the capitalist-driven economy, or its well-known post-capitalist varieties which are presented deceitfully as "planning."

How many hours of study, of reading, of reflection, do we

dedicate ourselves to each day? It is necessary, I would say, above all of our other obligations, to dedicate ourselves many hours a day because this concerns vital elements for this project. Sometimes we think that everything should be controlled from Caracas. No! It is about creating, as Mészáros says, a coordinated combination of parallel systems; from there comes the regionalization, the driving districts. We still haven't created a single one, and we have the law, we have our decree. But it was just a decree, and within the driving districts are the communes.

Occasionally we can fall into the illusion that by just calling something a certain name – I am against calling everything "socialist," socialist stadium, socialist avenue – what is a socialist avenue, kid! This is suspicious. Somebody wanted to call an avenue "socialist," socialist bakery, socialist Miraflores. This is suspect because one could be led to believe that okay, it's finished we called it socialist, and we're all done. Change the name, and that's it.

It's like the joke of the capybara and the Indians. A Spanish priest arrives – this was years ago, during the Holy Week – traveling along the plains through Indian lands. He comes to an indigenous town and the Indians are there, dancing and everything, they have their ways of celebrating, their own gods, their customs, and their food. So, the priest tells them, "You can't eat pork during Holy Week. On Holy Thursday you have to eat fish or capybara." And because there was a big fat pig there and the priest sensed what was waiting for him, he asked: "Do you understand?" "Yes, we understand." "You can't eat pork or meat from livestock." Then, before leaving, the priest brings them to the river to baptize them and he asks: "What are your names?" The Indian was named Caribay. "No, no, what is this Caribay? Your name is Juana. We must give people Christian names." And you, what is your name?" Another Indian name, Guaicaipuro. "No, what is this, give me a break Guaicaipuro, your name will be Nicolás." He left and when he came back on Holy Thursday, he saw that the Indians were dancing and roasting a pig. "How is it possible that you are going to eat this pig? I told you that you cannot eat pork!" So, one of the Cacique chiefs says: "No, we solved the problem. We baptized the pig and named it Capybara." They changed its name, they brought it to the river, they put it into the water. "Pig, your name is Capybara." And they ate the pig.

This is how we are with socialism: "Your name is socialism, kid," but you are still a pig deep down. I make these remarks, products of my reflections, after some study and comparisons with reality.

We must implement social ownership, the socialist spirit

Look at this view. This is the Mene Grande plant. Another plant could fit here. We will have to see what the surrounding land, Satellite Miranda, could produce. It seemed useless, just jungle and snakes. Each factory that we create should be able to start producing the day it is opened, for example, guava. Does this make sense? The plant should be on unproductive land and surely it is on national land, a thousand hectares of social property that can coexist with small property.

We must associate ourselves with the small producers, but we must insert social property, the spirit of socialism, throughout the entire chain, from agricultural work, where mangoes, guava, and strawberries are grown, to the distribution and consumption systems of the local producers.

We have done all of this in the interests of the transition. However, we should not lose sight, friends, of the core part of this project: We must not continue opening factories that are like islands, surrounded by the sea of capitalism, because the sea will swallow them up.

The same thing happens with housing. Where are the productive zones in Ciudad Caribia? We have created plenty of housing there, but I don't see the industrial zone. And I remember having said years ago, when we started there, and we went there, and we walked around. There is El Junquito, there is the sea. My God, here the night is nice and cool, great for tourism, there should already be some lodgings built.

Simón Bolívar said: "What we want will not come to us through divine intervention." There should already be a system of hotels there, restaurants with a view of the sea. There is a magic mountain there that I call the Wall. It is the Path of the Indians. What is it that Cipriano Castro said? "It is the insolent mark of the foreigner, the insolent mark of the Spanish invader, that they could never pass through this trail!" They never made it through this path.

I believe that you can even find human remains there, or remains of indigenous craftwork. That is why it is called the Path of the Indians, and the other one: the Path of the Spaniards, though this was Guaicaipuro's path. Not a single Spaniard passed through there, or we should say, in respect for modern-day Spain, not a single imperialist passed through.

These were the paths of Guaicaipuro, the road of heaven. It is made up of seven plateaus that can be seen clearly from above. So, look, this is really good for the cultivation of citrus. Citrus and flowers grow here. I even said they should build a terrace for the industrial zone. Where is the industrial zone? Did you see it? Where are the industries? There are none. That is in Ciudad Caribia, and I will be happy the day I see it.

Since the first day that we began to construct housing there, we should have begun. I even asked once why wait until the housing is built, since it is a long process? We are working on the transport and the roadways. What we are doing in Ciudad Caribia is a colossal undertaking, but why wait until it is all finished before we begin to plant the trees, the nurseries for the citrus fruits, flowers, urban agriculture, tubers?

Carayaca is near there; once we walked around and ended

up in Carayaca. Over there you can get to the Naval School, from behind, from the patio, but as far as I know, there isn't even a hectare yet, right?

Once when I wasn't in a big hurry I went there, via the Caracas-La Guaira Highway, with entrances and roads that go both places. Go there so you can see it.

I went and came across fields of tomatoes, and a man operating a water pump. I asked him, "Where do you extract the water?" "Over there under the ravine, on your right, as you go toward it, there is an opening there." I saw mango groves, grafted with those really big mangoes, and a litter of chickens on a small piece of land, peppers, etc. I asked the man: "Who owns all of this?" "Mister so and so." And how much does he pay you? "Well, sometimes he pays us, and sometimes he doesn't." See? They are exploited on these small farms.

Recently we inaugurated the Mamera-El Junquito Highway. Tell me if you have seen a farm there, a collective one. I remember I went there three years ago, and the first image that I had was of the great potential, of the beautiful land, the beautiful hills, the beautiful climate. We have finished the highway and yet there is not a single productive unit there that we have created ourselves.

It was our belief that the highway was the main objective. Will the railroad be our goal? Will the highway be our goal? Or, in terms of the central concept, do we turn the entire geographic-human socio-territorial and cultural relation around? A change is clearly necessary, but sometimes we don't want to understand, and not just sometimes, we almost never understand it.

The objective is the people

You remember, Jacqueline Faría, it seems like a hundred years ago you were the president of Hidrocapital and I, watching television, saw that you were in the Cota 905 putting in water pipes, and I called you. I barely knew you, and I said, "Doctor, engineer

Jacqueline, what project is accompanying the main idea of the pipe? Is it just the pipe? And those shanties alongside the site, does anyone see them? Is the pipe the objective? Is the objective the oil pipeline? Or is it an instrument? Is the highway the objective?" I could go on and on.

Once we came with [Ramon] Carrizales. I remember that he was the Minister of Transport and Infrastructure. We were coming from Elorza heading toward Mantecal in some helicopters and I saw that they were still working on the highways. I told him, let's land there, between Mantecal and Elorza. I asked the workers, "Where do you live?" "Mantecal, Elorza." "How many of you have your own house?" Almost none of them. "What kind of housing do you have?" A shack. I remember that I said to Carrizales, "hey, it would be great to make a sketch." Look, this is Elorza, Mantecal and the highway, thousands and thousands of hectares cross this highway, and it turns out that the very workers who are working on the highway don't have housing.

I asked some engineers who were there, "How many houses fit in a hectare?" Let's say ten hectares, 800 houses, simple ones, not big buildings or anything, so taking advantage of the impulse, as they say, with the machinery used for the highway, millions of bolívares, technicians, engineers, the very same workers who didn't have housing could have built a residential area for themselves.

This is not the same as simply finishing the highway. When their work is over, what awaits those workers? The majority of them end up damaging the highway so that they can return to work on the same highway. That is how they pass their lives. Surrounded by land on all sides, they finish their lives without a home, and they leave their children homeless. I would take up that little town of ten hectares and maybe on this side a hundred more hectares, livestock, agriculture. The highway, from the capitalist point of view, who benefits most from the highway? The large estate owner can now ship more livestock at lower costs.

Putting your feet on the ground would probably be beneficial, because if you have a bicycle, an old one, you can travel by bicycle along the highway in bits and pieces to get to the next town, or you can walk along the highway. This is the benefit for the exploited of having one's feet on the ground. On the other hand, someone who has a small herd of animals, a farm, and a few trucks, that person will benefit a million times more than the person with their feet on the ground.

Therefore, in terms of the highway, from a traditional point of view, we are actually making the rift wider. It seems that we often don't even realize how to find the right formula.

What I am doing is organizing my reflections so that you can make adjustments to what you are working on, and so that you work together and communicate as a team, and we can all give everything the utmost importance, as small as it may be. Even if it is a little project over there in a small town in Mérida. Not just, "This is a trout farm." What else is there? As small as it is, we must give it this character.

I believe that over these years we have accumulated experience. We have created entities that did not exist before. I believe that we have ended up accumulating resources, investing resources and we will continue to do so. I believe we have new codes. I believe we have a new legal framework, starting with the Constitution. We have laws for communal councils, the law for the developmental initiative districts, but those of us responsible for enforcing them haven't paid any attention to these laws.

I hope to see answers to these reflections and to this public self-criticism that I am making.

Greater efficiency for better results

And you, my dear friends, ministers, those who prefer to work alone, you tell me. I have the power to do what the law requires. In this, I have no discretion. I shouldn't have it with anyone, because sometimes there is jealousy, and I have come across ministers or vice-ministers who get jealous.

You are all obliged to keep me informed, not to be quiet. If any of you see that within a certain ministry, or other entity, there is an exclusive clique forming, tell me because I have the power that the Constitution gives me, a power that no one else has, and I will shoot a missile at them. You can't do it, but I can, and I will do it with pleasure. Believe me, I will do it with pleasure.

It is sad that we stay quiet, so we are not seen in a bad light. We are not second-grade students, nor are we in elementary school. This is the revolutionary government of Venezuela, ratified by the people two weeks ago, but also highly criticized by the people and with reason, and these reasons are based on our lack of efficiency.

I read somewhere, and it has been mentioned before, but since there are various ministry councils with various phases, it is possible that some of you haven't heard me say this, or maybe you understand it better than I do: A team that does not communicate, or a team that communicates badly, will not amount to much.

We need a level of communication, coordination, a crossing, or an intersection of plans, of diagnosis, of problems, of coordinated action. It's like a war. What would the infantry do without the tanks? And what would the armored division do without the infantry or the marines without the army? What does a male do alone, or a female alone, or night without day, or the root by itself, or the branches on their own? We are nothing without integrating our vision in our work, in everything. It will be hard, but we will persevere.

That is why I ask you. I ask Nicolás who will now step up to take on the role of vice president, and the newly arrived ministers as well as those who are staying, to make a bigger effort, to give a little more. I will do my part as well. I will be involved in everything.

Strengthening of the National System of Public Media

Another criticism, and I hope that no one feels bad about it. I won't name anyone, but recently, as always, I have been watching TV. I watch a few programs on our channel, the channel of all of Venezuela, and it seems as if we will persist in clinging to the past, giving a voice to those who barely have anything to say to the country, airing their videos. Is this the most important thing right now? What about the government's management? Why not have programs with workers? Where can we voice our self-criticisms? We should not be afraid to criticize, nor to self-criticize. We need it. It gives us nourishment.

I imagine, for example, my dear Vanessa in the Copelia factory speaking at length with experts, dedicating an hour to them. I imagine my dear Mario over there in the Cerro Azul plant. Even if it is eleven at night, it doesn't matter – interviewing workers, walking around the factory, looking at the cement, being shown around.

Four hours on a Saturday isn't enough. This must be a systematic plan, permanent, continuous, etc.

And not just on channel eight, no, on every channel. I often watch TVes, they have good documentaries, and Vive as well, but I have the impression that each channel does its own thing. We don't really have, although we like to talk about it, a National Public Media System, we don't.

Ernesto [Villegas], convert yourself into the leader of this system. Create it, we will create it together. It will include, finally like a system, connectivity with other systems, or subsystems, community media and popular media. It's like the story I told you of the bugle and the horse: Local television, local newspapers, international news, Telesur; each one is on its own. This is the truth.

I am sure that this is how it is. There is no National Public Media System, we don't have one. We will create it. We have the instruments to do so. What we lack is the will and, maybe, obviously, the capacity. But if we take the risk, we will do it. It is necessary.

Glossary

Aló Presidente ("Hello, Mr. President"). A weekly talk show that ran from 1999–2012, hosted by then-president Hugo Chávez and filmed in various locations. Over the course of the show, he would take calls from viewers, debate with government officials, or discuss topics ranging from geography, to history, to pedagogy.

Amphictyonic Congress of Panama. A congress organized by Simón Bolívar in 1826, aimed at bringing together the republics of Latin America in solidarity and defense against Spain. Attendees included Gran Colombia (what is now Colombia, Ecuador, Panama, and Venezuela), Peru, the United Provinces of Central America (Guatemala, El Salvador, Honduras, Nicaragua, and Costa Rica), and Mexico.

Atahualpa (1502–1533). The last Inca emperor. He was captured by conquistador Francisco Pizzaro, and executed by strangulation. His death marked the beginning of the fall of the Inca Empire and the rise of European colonization on the continent.

Augusto C. Sandino (1895–1934). A farmer, mining engineer, and revolutionary political leader who led the Army for the Defense of Nicaraguan National Sovereignty (EDSN) in 1927, and drove out US military forces from Nicaragua in 1933. He was assassinated a year later, and is the namesake of the Nicaraguan revolutionary movement, the Sandinistas.

Bandung Conference (Asian-African Conference). A conference held in Bandung, Indonesia in 1955 that hosted representatives from 29 governments of Asian and African nations (many newly independent) to promote economic and cultural cooperation and to oppose colonialism and neocolonialism. The conference was a key point in the eventual creation of the Non-Aligned Movement.

Bernardo O'Higgins Riquelme (1778-1842). A Chilean independence leader and one of the commanders who led the army to victory against Spanish rule. He was the first Supreme Director of Chile to lead a fully independent Chilean state, establishing libraries, hospitals, and schools (even proposing abolishing the nobility before he was deposed by the ruling class) – and thus considered one of the country's founding fathers.

Bolivarian Alternative for Latin America (ALBA). Founded in 2004 with an agreement between presidents Hugo Chávez of Venezuela and Fidel Castro of Cuba, is a regional platform that proposes a process of regional integration through strengthening political unity, promoting and working toward the program of 21st Century Socialism, defending national sovereignty against US interventions, and working to address poverty, illiteracy, and the rights of indigenous and marginalized populations. ALBA is considered to be instrumental in blocking the realization of the FTAA and continues to drive efforts to lessen the grip of US imperialism in the region.

Cacique Guaicaipuro (1530-1568). A cacique (chief) who resisted Spanish invasion into what is now Caracas, Venezuela. He formed an alliance with other Indigenous leaders, successfully keeping the colonizers at bay until the Battle of Maracapana in 1568. He refused to surrender when Spanish soldiers set his house on fire, where he died. Today, he is one of the most celebrated Indigenous leaders of Venezuela.

Cilia Adela Flores de Maduro (1956-). A Venezuelan lawyer and politician. She served as deputy and eventually president of the National Assembly of Venezuela. She is currently First Lady and married to president of Venezuela Nicolás Maduro.

Communal Council. Deliberative bodies where local community representatives propose, discuss and decide on public projects and initiatives and address issues the community is facing.

Communal councils encompass from 200 to 400 families in urban areas or 20 to 50 families in rural areas. There are over 47,000 registered communal councils in Venezuela.

Erika del Valle Farías Peña (1972–). A Venezuelan politician who served as Minister for the Office of the Presidency three times: as Minister for Urban Agriculture, Minister for the Communes, and as deputy to the 2017 National Constituent Assembly. She is a militant and a member of the National Directorate of the United Socialist Party of Venezuela (PSUV).

Ezequiel Zamora (1817–1860). A leader of the Federalists in the Venezuelan Federal War. He was known as *General del Pueblo Soberano* (General of the Sovereign People) and for his slogan, "*Tierra y hombres libres!*" (Land and free people!).

Farmapatria. A Venezuelan state-owned company, attached to the Ministry of Health. Its creation was made official in 2012, Farmapatria created and manages a network of pharmacies that sell medicines at subsidized prices at national grocery and convenience stores.

Fidel Castro (1926-2016). One of the leaders of the 1959 Cuban Revolution and the President of Cuba for 32 years. Castro and Chávez developed a close bond as both political allies and personal comrades and friends. Chávez was invited to Havana by Castro after he was released from prison in 1994 and received essential medical care in Cuba toward the end of his life.

Francisco de Miranda (1750–1816). A Venezuelan revolutionary leader. He dreamed of a united and independent South America, and while his military pursuits toward that end failed, he paved the way for his country's independence – he is often considered the "precursor" to Simón Bolivar, with whom he helped establish the First Republic of Venezuela.

Francisco de Paula Santander (1792–1840). A Colombian military and political leader during the 1810–1819 independence war of the United Provinces of New Granada (present-day Colombia). He fought alongside Simón Bolívar for independence from Spain, and later served as the acting president of Gran Colombia, and again later as the president of the Republic of New Granada.

Free Trade Area of the Americas (FTAA). A trade agreement proposed in 1994 by US president Bill Clinton that would eliminate trade barriers between the US and all countries of the Americas, excluding Cuba. This would effectively create a US-led economic bloc against Cuba, prevent regional integration, and facilitate neoliberal imposition across the continent. It was strongly opposed by popular movements across the region, and Venezuelan president Hugo Chávez was one of its most vocal critics. Negotiations failed to reach an agreement and ended in failure in 2005.

José Francisco Morazán Quesada (1792–1842). A politician and general. He believed in Central America as a progressive and united nation, serving as the last president of the Federal Republic of Central America (a territory of what is now Costa Rica, El Salvador, Guatemala, Honduras, and Nicaragua as well as the southern Mexican state of Chiapas) before its dissolution.

João Goulart (1919–1976). The 24th president of Brazil, commonly nicknamed Jango. In 1964, he proposed *Reformas Basicas* (Basic Reforms) that would institute educational reforms to combat adult illiteracy, tax reforms to redirect income from multinational corporations to the country, land reforms, among others. Seventeen days later he was overthrown in a military coup.

João Pedro Stedile (1953–). One of the co-founders of the *Movimento dos Trabalhadores Rurais Sem Terra* (Landless Workers' Movement), a movement of rural workers fighting for land reform and against social inequality. It is one of the largest mass social movements in South America.

José Carlos Mariátegui (1894– 1930). A journalist and one of the most influential socialist thinkers of Latin America. His most famous book *Seven Interpretive Essays on Peruvian Reality*, translated and reprinted many times since its first publication in 1928, is considered a landmark in the analysis of the culture, politics, and economy of Peru.

José de San Martín (1778–1850). An Argentine soldier and statesman, who helped lead the revolutions against Spanish rule in Argentina, Chile, and Peru; serving for a time as Protector of Peru. He is regarded as a national hero in these countries.

José Gervasio Artigas (1764–1850). An Uruguayan political leader, and one of the principal figures in the Spanish-American wars of independence. He is regarded as a national hero in Uruguay.

José Inácio de Abreu e Lima (1794–1869). A Brazilian military officer who served as one of the generals of Simón Bolívar during the Spanish–American wars of independence.

José Martí (1853–1895). Known as Cuba's national hero. He was a revolutionary leader for Cuban independence from Spanish colonial rule and looming US expansion. While spent mostly in exile, Martí dedicated his life to uniting and preparing pro-independent forces and organizing the Cuban Revolutionary Party.

Juan Velasco Alvarado (1910–1977). The president of Peru following a successful coup against his predecessor. He implemented a number of progressive measures, limiting US economic influence; nationalizing transportation, communications, and electricity; and redistributing land. He was overthrown in a coup by his prime minister.

Luis Carlos Prestes (1898–1990). A senator and the leader of the Brazilian Communist Party. In 1924, he notably led a three-year trek through the countryside in an attempt to spark rebellion. While it failed, he became a hero and was known as a charismatic leader of the left in South America.

Manuela Sáenz (1797–1856). A key figure in the Spanish-American wars of independence by gathering information, distributing leaflets, serving in the cavalry, and distributing medicine during battles. She was also Simón Bolívar's long-time lover and saved him from assassination, earning herself the title

Glossary

"*Libertadora del Libertador*" ("liberator of the liberator").

Mission Barrio Adentro. A social welfare program started by Hugo Chávez aimed at providing low-cost, high-quality medical care to the working class and poor. The initiative was supported by Cuban doctors who helped supply medical support.

Movimento dos Trabalhadores Rurais Sem Terra (Landless Workers' Movement) (MST). First established in 1984, the MST has grown to a membership of over 1.5 million rural workers and farmers and over 7.5 hectares of land won through occupation campaigns. The MST focuses on land distribution and agroecology and advocates for a program of popular agrarian reform, but as a social mass movement, also organizes for the liberation of all people, including Afro–Brazilians, LGBTQ populations, and indigenous people.

Non-Aligned Movement (NAM). Founded during the collapse of the colonial system and the independence struggles of the peoples of Africa, Asia, Latin America and other regions of the world and at the height of the Cold War. The Non-Aligned Movement held its first conference (the Belgrade Conference) in 1961 under the leadership of Josip Broz Tito of Yugoslavia, Gamal Abdel Nasser of Egypt, Jawaharlal Nehru of India, Kwame Nkrumah of Ghana, and Sukarno of Indonesia.

The Organization of American States (OAS). An international organization formed in Bogotá, Colombia in 1948 by the United States and its allies. Though the OAS Charter invokes the rhetoric of multilateralism and cooperation, the organization has been used as a tool to fight against communism in the hemisphere and to impose a US agenda on the countries of the Americas. The OAS has participated in the overthrow of governments that attempt to exercise their legitimate sovereignty, including Cuba, Honduras, Bolivia, Nicaragua, Venezuela, and Haiti.

PDVAL (Venezuelan Production and Distribution of Food). The national food supply network of Venezuela, founded in 2008 in response to the stockpiling in the private sector driving up prices of basic goods. PDVAL distributes food, cleaning, personal hygiene, and household products, as well as any other product for human use and consumption, throughout the national territory at fair prices.

PDVSA (Petroleum of Venezuela). The state-owned oil and gas company of Venezuela founded in 1976. The PDVSA has been the target of US sanctions since 2017, blocking its access to international credit and financial institutions.

PSUV (United Socialist Party of Venezuela). Founded in 2006 on the initiative of Hugo Chávez after his victory in the Presidential elections, the PSUV is a unification of pro-Bolivarian Revolution forces, representing over a million active members participating in many levels of society. Currently, the PSUV is the ruling party in Venezuela, with Nicolas Maduro as President.

Rafael Urdaneta (1788–1845). A Venezuelan general and hero of the Spanish-American wars of independence. He also served as president of Gran Colombia and was one of Simón Bolívar's closest allies.

Simón Bolívar (1783–1830). A Venezuelan who is known as *El Libertador* (*Liberator of America*) for his leadership in liberating Colombia, Venezuela, Ecuador, Peru, Panama, and Bolivia from Spanish rule. He served as president of Gran Colombia, Peru, and Bolivia.

Simón Rodríguez (1769–1854). A Venezuelan educator and teacher who was a mentor to Simón Bolívar. When exiled for a failed attempt at liberating Venezuela, he went by Simon Robinson and traveled the United States and France, eventually returning to South America.

Tomás Borge Martínez (1930–2012). A writer, politician, and cofounder of the Sandinista National Liberation Front (FSLN) in Nicaragua. He also served as Interior Minister of Nicaragua, and held the titles of "Vice-Secretary and President of the FSLN." Borge was also a member of the Nicaraguan Parliament and National Congress, and Ambassador to Peru.

Túpac Katari (c. 1750–1781). An Aymara leader of the resistance against Spanish colonialism in what is now Bolivia. He built an army of about 40,000 men and laid siege to the colonists in La Paz in 1781, alongside his wife Bartonlina Sisa and his sister Gregoria Apaza. That same year, he was executed by the Spanish loyalists by quartering.

Venezolanidad. A feeling of national and cultural belonging with the Venezuelan land and nation, carrying with it a sense of pride regarding the independence process from the Spanish colonizers, and an ongoing commitment to national sovereignty.

World Social Forum (WSF). An annual meeting of civil society organizations founded in 2001. The first iteration of the WSF, held in Porto Alegre, Brazil, raised the slogan "Another World is Possible" as a challenge to the neoliberal agenda of the World Economic Forum.

Contributors

CARLOS RON is the President of the Simón Bolívar Institute for Peace and Solidarity Among Peoples, and serves as the Vice-minister of Foreign Affairs for North America.

HUGO CHÁVEZ (1954-2013) was President of Venezuela and leader of the Bolivarian Revolution. He nationalized key industries, used oil revenues for social programs for the poor, and passed important reforms in the fields of health, housing, and education.

JORGE ARREAZA is the Minister of Popular Power (and Vice President of the PSUV VP) for Communes and Social Movements. He served as Vice President of Venezuela from 2013 to 2016, and as Foreign Minister from 2017-2021.

MANOLO DE LOS SANTOS is the co-executive director of the People's Forum and is a researcher at Tricontinental: Institute for Social Research. He co-edited, most recently, *Viviremos: Venezuela vs. Hybrid War* (LeftWord Books/1804 Books, 2020) and *Comrade of the Revolution: Selected Speeches of Fidel Castro* (LeftWord Books/1804 Books, 2021). He is a co-coordinator of the People's Summit for Democracy.

VIJAY PRASHAD is an Indian historian and journalist. Prashad is the author of forty books, including *Washington Bullets*, *Red Star Over the Third World*, *The Darker Nations: A People's History of the Third World* and *The Poorer Nations: A Possible*

History of the Global South. He is the Chief Correspondent for Globetrotter and editor at LeftWord Books. He has appeared in two films – *Shadow World* (2016) and *Two Meetings* (2017).

CPSIA information can be obtained
at www.ICGtesting.com
Printed in the USA
JSHW010302230123
36595JS00004B/17